解码中华文化基因

Decoding the Culture Genes of China

秦瑜明 ◎ 主编

白晓晴　张　龙 ◎ 执行主编

中国传媒大学出版社
·北京·

图书在版编目(CIP)数据

解码中华文化基因 / 秦瑜明主编；白晓晴，张龙执行主编. -- 北京：中国传媒大学出版社，2023.9
ISBN 978-7-5657-3458-8

Ⅰ. ①解… Ⅱ. ①秦… ②白… ③张… Ⅲ. ①中华文化—介绍 Ⅳ. ①K203

中国国家版本馆 CIP 数据核字(2023)第 149233 号

解码中华文化基因
JIEMA ZHONGHUA WENHUA JIYIN

主　　　编	秦瑜明
执 行 主 编	白晓晴　张　龙
特约策划编辑	秦瑜明　白晓晴
责 任 编 辑	周　娜
封 面 设 计	拓美设计
责 任 印 制	李志鹏

出版发行	中国传媒大学出版社
社　　址	北京市朝阳区定福庄东街 1 号	邮　编	100024
电　　话	86-10-65450528　65450532	传　真	65779405
网　　址	http://cucp.cuc.edu.cn
经　　销	全国新华书店
印　　刷	北京中科印刷有限公司
开　　本	889mm×1194mm　1/16
印　　张	16.75
字　　数	264 千字
版　　次	2023 年 9 月第 1 版
印　　次	2023 年 9 月第 1 次印刷
书　　号	ISBN 978-7-5657-3458-8/K · 3458	定　价	198.00 元

本社法律顾问：北京嘉润律师事务所　郭建平

序

中国是一个团结统一的多民族国家。中华优秀传统文化是中国各民族在五千多年发展进程中存在过的物质、制度和精神方面的文化总和，包含语言文字、文学艺术、工匠技艺、传统习俗和生活方式等诸多方面的内容。中华文化基因源于中华优秀传统文化，是中华民族在世世代代的生产生活中传承并发展的基本文化因素，包含着中华民族建构的礼乐、仁义、中和、民本、家国、天下、王道、大同、天人合一等思想理念。中华文化基因为中国多民族的生存与发展提供了巨大的精神支撑和强大的内在动力，对于建设中华民族共有的精神家园发挥着极其重要的作用。

习近平总书记指出，以铸牢中华民族共同体意识为主线，全面推进民族团结进步事业，激发全民族文化创新创造活力，增强实现中华民族伟大复兴的精神力量。中华民族的精神力量源自中华民族五千多年历史所孕育的中华优秀传统文化，根植于中国特色社会主义的伟大实践。要激发全民族文化创新创造活力，实现中华民族的伟大复兴，就要对中华文化基因进行提炼解码，形成各民族人心凝聚、团结奋进的强大精神纽带，更要对中华文化基因进行创新传播，使之与时代发展同频共振，以中华文明的文化精髓为中国式现代化发展提供智慧源泉。

在当今信息化和全球化的时代，在各民族群体中开展中华优秀传统文化的传播，对于永续中华民族的根与魂、铸牢中华民族共同体意识、建设社会主义文化强国具有重要意义。尤其是对于青年人来说，只有具有了对中华文化基因充分的认知和理解，懂得自己文化的传统、价值和发展方向，才能拥有信心和力量，成为具有民族情怀和时代精神并可以担负传承中华文化使命的新一代。

《解码中华文化基因》融合出版物通过讲述中国历史发展进程中的各类文化遗产故事，呈现出了这些文化遗产背后的中华文化的精神内涵、内在意味与核心价值。剪纸、年画、面人、绢花，呈现出中国人对平安、团圆的强烈愿望，这是老百姓最普遍、最本质的愿望；中国画、书法、篆刻，展现的是中国人在文化生活中的性情志向、审美素养；太极拳、中医、围棋，展现出中国人顺应自然、追求人与自然和谐共生的人生智慧；古琴、酿酒、制茶，营造出一种诗意的氛围，体现了中国人对于日常生活审美化的追求。通过器物、技艺、艺术作品讲述出来的中华文化，有内在的精神，有活的灵魂。通过视听图文的融媒体语言感知这些内容，能够使读者了解历史上中华民族如何享受有情致的人生，如何创造有意义的生活，从而对中华文化有更全面的认知。

中华优秀传统文化的创新性传播必定是传承历史、观照当下和面向未来的。本书试图以现代的眼光去审视中华传统文化，注重传承、弘扬那些既能代表优秀传统文化，又有助于当代文化创新发展的精神内涵。只有回归到传统文化中反观我们的日常生活，才能显现中华文化的本来面貌，才能深化大众对中华文化的根基意识，从而增强文化自觉、坚定文化自信，使中国人民以强烈的历史主动精神积极投身于社会主义文化强国的建设中。

以融合出版物形态呈现中华文化的基因密码，是中国传媒大学铸牢中华民族共同体意识研究基地的创新探索。研究基地致力于开展以融合传播铸牢中华民族共同体意识的理论研究与实践探索，通过中华优秀传统文化融合出版模式的创新，积极顺应媒体融合纵深发展趋势，助力建构数字时代新型出版传播体系，为夯实中华民族共同体意识的思想文化基础、建设中华民族共有精神家园提供有力支撑。

期待海内外读者通过阅读此书，不仅可以收获中华传统文化知识，也可以在生动的融媒体表达中体会中华民族的伟大生命力和创造力，感受到中国人独具的性格、灵魂和情致，从而加深对中华优秀传统文化的认知与理解。期待青年读者通过阅读此书，能够涵养情怀、修身明志，进而担负起传承和弘扬中华优秀传统文化的历史使命。

由于中华文化基因在范畴、维度和标准上存在诸多认识和理解上的差异，对其进行融媒诠释与创新呈现具有一定的挑战性。《解码中华文化基因》是数字媒体与纸质媒体深度连接、图文与视频高度联动的融合出版创新产品，希望能够获得广大读者尤其是青年读者的喜爱。

2023 年 6 月

张树庭

Foreword

China is a united country with multiple ethnic groups. Developed by the multi-ethnic Chinese nation over the past five thousand years, the fine traditional Chinese culture encompasses not only material culture, but also nonmaterial aspects such as institutions, beliefs and values. Originating from the fine traditional Chinese culture, Chinese cultural genes, as the fundamental cultural elements inherited and developed by the Chinese nation, have been strong spiritual pillars and momentum for the survival and development of China's various ethnic groups, playing an essential role in the construction of a shared spiritual home for the Chinese nation.

The Chinese nation's powerful source of inspiration lies in the fine traditional Chinese culture that has been developed for over five thousand years, as well as in the socialist culture with Chinese characteristics. To ignite the cultural creativity of the entire nation, and to realize the great rejuvenation of the Chinese nation, it is necessary to collect and refine the defining symbols and best elements of Chinese culture and to decode these Chinese cultural genes, so as to form a strong spiritual bond for Chinese people of all ethnic groups. It is also necessary to disseminate these Chinese cultural genes in an innovative way that reflects the development of the modern society, which can provide an example of a Chinese path to modernization.

In the global information age, the dissemination of fine traditional Chinese culture among China's various ethnic groups helps sustain the roots and soul of the Chinese people. It also helps forge a strong sense of community for the Chinese nation and turn China into a country with a strong socialist culture. It particularly benefits China's young people, who will gain more confidence and strength to carry forward China's cultural heritage when they are equipped with more knowledge of Chinese cultural genes and understand better the traditions, values and future of the fine Chinese culture.

This convergent publishing product *Decoding the Culture Genes of China* presents China's various types of cultural heritages, conveying the spirits, connotation and core values of the Chinese culture. For instance, Chinese paper cutting, *nianhua* (New Year prints), dough figurines and silk flowers demonstrate Chinese people's desires for safety and family reunion; Chinese painting, calligraphy and seal engraving embody Chinese artists' self-cultivation of mind and disposition; Tai Chi Quan, traditional Chinese medicine and the game of Go impart the Chinese wisdom of harmonious coexistence between man and nature; whereas *guqin*, *baijiu* (Chinese white liquor) distilling and tea-making, which create a poetic atmosphere, convey Chinese people's pursuit of an aesthetic daily life. Through these artifacts, craftsmanship and artworks, stories of Chinese culture are told vividly in multimedia language which integrates graphics, text, audio and video, enabling readers to experience the aesthetic and meaningful life of the Chinese people and to obtain a more comprehensive understanding of the Chinese culture.

To innovatively disseminate the fine traditional Chinese culture means carrying forward the past while reflecting upon the present and the future. This book attempts to examine traditional Chinese culture from a modern perspective, promoting Chinese spirits that not only represent the essence of fine traditional culture but also benefit the development of contemporary culture. To reflect on our daily life in light of the tradition can deepen our understanding of the Chinese culture and of our roots, helping to build a stronger sense of cultural confidence throughout our nation, and motivating us to undertake the task of turning China into a country with a strong socialist culture.

This convergent publishing product which presents Chinese cultural genes, symbolizes an innovation effort made by the Research Base for Forging a Strong Sense of Community for the Chinese Nation. The Research Base has been exploring innovative modes of publishing materials about fine traditional Chinese culture, which conforms to the new trend of media convergence and contributes to the construction of a new publishing system in the digital age. Building a strong cultural foundation to help forge a strong sense of community for the Chinese nation, the Research Base is also promoting the construction of a shared spiritual home for the whole nation.

Hopefully, the convergent publishing product *Decoding the Culture Genes of China* can equip readers with knowledge about Chinese culture, enabling them to experience the vitality and creativity of the Chinese nation, and deepening their understanding of the fine traditional Chinese culture. It is also hoped that through reading this book, young readers can nurture their minds and aspirations, shouldering the mission of carrying forward fine traditional Chinese culture.

As there is no uniform definition of Chinese cultural genes, it has been quite a challenging task to try to present them through a convergent publishing product. However, *Decoding the Culture Genes of China* represents a fine example of in-depth convergence of digital and print media as well as innovative integration of graphics, texts and videos. Hopefully, the book can be well received, especially by young readers.

June 2023

Zhang Shuting

前　言

中华文明绵延数千年，有其独特的价值体系。中华优秀传统文化植根于中国人内心，潜移默化地影响着中国人的思维和行为方式。对中华文化基因进行解码转化与创新传播、对中华优秀传统文化进行创造性转化和创新性发展，有助于引导全国各族人民树立正确的历史观、民族观和文化观，推进中华民族共有的精神家园建设。

为了提升中华文化的传播力和影响力，焕发中华文化基因在当代文化生活中的生命力，中国传媒大学开展了"解码中华文化基因"项目，选取我国最具代表性的文化遗产，编创60集中英文短视频，通过中国新闻社面向海内外传播。项目成果着重讲述各民族文化遗产的历史来源、发展演变、当代价值、当地民俗、传承形态、匠人逸事等，创新传统文化叙事方式，通过短小精湛的文化遗产故事传达文化内涵与价值观念。在媒体融合纵深发展的趋势下，中国传媒大学数字出版师生团队将中英双语的图文、视频结集成册，编创《解码中华文化基因》融合出版物，服务于文化普及、高校美育、课外阅读、英语学习等各类使用场景，旨在拓展数字文化传播空间、打造融合出版新模式、服务线上线下阅读场景，以推动中华优秀传统文化的大众化、常态化、长效化传播。

《解码中华文化基因》融合出版物根据文化遗产的技艺类型、表现形式、产品形态，将60个主题分为四方之艺、别具匠心、妙手丹青和精雕细琢四个篇章。其中，四方之艺篇以表演艺术、传统游艺、传统体育为主要内容，展现了历史上中华民族的精神风貌；别具匠心篇包含传统美食、地域建筑、劳动生活等领域的非遗技艺，凸显了中国历史上劳动人民的智慧与匠心；妙手丹青篇主要介绍传统美术、民族服饰、工艺品等文化遗产，体现出了中华文化遗产的美学追求和艺术造诣；精雕细琢篇则以手工艺为主，包含雕刻雕塑、编织刺绣等，使读者能够感受到手工艺人"以形写神"的创造力。

　　本书对文化类出版物的融合形态进行了一定的创新探索。一是注重媒体融合，增强阅读体验。在文字阅读的基础上，本书嵌入了中英文视频二维码，读者能够通过扫码的方式进入视频呈现的交互程序，在图、文、声、像、影的立体化表达中体验中华文化遗产故事，获得更强的互动参与感。二是创新版面设计，突出视觉吸引力。本书运用海报式章节设计，将各文化遗产主题融入年轻化、国潮化的版面设计中，使读者在阅读本书时能够直观感受到中华优秀传统文化的生动样貌。三是契合移动传播，推出竖屏短视频。本书所呈现的短视频作品采用竖屏构图，便于读者翻阅书籍时使用手机扫码观看，同时，视频充分整合CG动画、三维建模、数码手绘等技术手段，对文化遗产进行了数字化还原和创意化再现，突出主题思想的同时也增强了中华传统文化的艺术感染力。

　　《解码中华文化基因》的编创是一次对中华传统文化内容进行融合出版的前沿探索。未来，我们还将进一步拓展中华文化基因的融媒传播与融合出版模式，树立和突出各民族共享的中华文化符号和中华文化形象，为各民族的交往、交流、交融提供新的路径与可能性。欢迎广大读者提出宝贵意见，我们将不断总结优化，使《解码中华文化基因》系列出版物日臻完善。

2023 年 6 月

Preface

The Chinese civilization, which has lasted for thousands of years, possesses a unique value system. The fine traditional Chinese culture is deeply rooted in the hearts of the Chinese people, subtly affecting their way of thinking and behavior. Decoding the genes of the Chinese culture and disseminate them innovatively, so as to creatively transform and develop China's fine traditional culture, will help guide Chinese people of all ethnic groups to establish proper views on history, nationality and culture, and promote the construction of a shared spiritual home for the Chinese nation.

To extend the reach and appeal of Chinese civilization, and to rejuvenate the vitality of Chinese cultural genes in the contemporary cultural life, the Communication University of China launched the project "Decoding the Culture Genes of China", producing short videos (in both Mandarin Chinese and English) which feature 60 China's representative cultural heritage items, and presented the videos in China and abroad through China News Service. These short videos focus on the historical origins, development, contemporary values, local folklore, and anecdotes of artisans of the cultural heritages of China's various ethnic groups, telling stories about traditional culture in an innovative way and conveying the cultural connotations and values through these short yet fascinating stories. In the trend of media convergence, the digital publishing faculty and students of the Communication University of China have compiled the bilingual texts, illustrations and videos of this project into this digital publishing product *Decoding the Culture Genes of China*, which can be used in various scenarios such as cultural popularization, aesthetic education in universities, extracurricular reading and English language learning. This product aims to expand the space for digital cultural dissemination, to create a new mode of convergent publishing, to serve both online and offline reading scenarios, as well as to promote a more extensive, regular and long-term dissemination of the fine traditional Chinese culture.

As the 60 cultural heritage items involve different types of skills, forms of expression and cultural products, the convergent publishing product *Decoding the Culture Genes of China* is divided into four chapters including Artistry, Ingenuity, Virtuosity and Craftsmanship. The chapter "Artistry" focuses on performing arts, traditional games and sports, showing the spirit of the Chinese nation throughout history. The chapter "Ingenuity" contains intangible cultural heritages in the fields of traditional cuisine, regional architecture and working life, highlighting the wisdom and ingenuity of the working people in Chinese history. The chapter "Virtuosity" introduces cultural heritage such as traditional fine arts, costumes and artifacts, reflecting the aesthetic pursuits and artistic attainment of the Chinese people. The chapter "Craftsmanship" focuses on handicrafts such as carving, sculpture, weaving and embroidery, enabling readers to experience the creativity of the artisans who "express the intangible through the tangible".

This book also symbolizes an effort in exploring innovative convergent forms of cultural publications. Firstly, through media convergence, the book enhances the readers' reading experience. Apart from texts, the book also contains QR codes of the Chinese and English short videos, so that the readers can scan the codes to enter into the interactive program of video presentation and experience the stories of the Chinese cultural heritage in the three-dimensional expression of graphics, text, audio and video, gaining a stronger sense of interactive participation. Secondly, the innovative layout design helps enhance the visual appeal. With the chapters designed in a poster style, the book integrates the various themes of cultural heritage into a youthful and trendy layout design, so that readers can immerse themselves in the fine traditional Chinese culture while reading the book. Thirdly, the short videos are mobile-friendly, as they are styled to fit the vertical screen of the mobile phone. While flipping through the book, readers can use their mobile phones to scan the QR codes and watch the vertical videos conveniently. In addition, the videos also integrate CG animation, 3D modelling, digital hand-drawing and other technical means to digitally restore and creatively reproduce the cultural heritage, highlighting the themes and enhancing the artistic impact of Chinese traditional culture.

The creation and production of the product *Decoding the Culture Genes of China* represents a cutting-edge exploration of convergent publishing of traditional Chinese cultural content. In the future, we will further expand the mode of convergent media dissemination and convergent publishing of Chinese cultural genes, establish and highlight Chinese cultural symbols and images shared by all ethnic groups, and provide new paths and possibilities for the communication and exchanges among various ethnic groups. We welcome valuable comments from our readers. And we will continue to optimize the *Decoding the Culture Genes of China* series to make it better.

June 2023

四方之艺

古 琴 /3
Guqin /5

太极拳 /7
Tai Chi Quan /9

京 剧 /11
Peking/Beijing Opera /13

昆 曲 /15
Kunqu Opera /17

皮影戏 /19
Chinese Shadow Puppetry /21

泉州南音 /23
Quanzhou *Nanyin* /25

围 棋 /27
The Game of Go /29

象 棋 /31
Xiangqi/the Chinese Chess /33

龙 舞 /35
Dragon Dance /37

狮 舞 /39
Lion Dance /41

口 技 /43
Oral Stunts /45

高 跷 /47
Stilts /49

秧 歌 /51
Yangko Dance (Sidling Songs) /53

抖空竹 /55
Diabolo Playing /57

传统箭术 /59
Traditional Archery /61

提线木偶戏 /63
Quanzhou String Puppet Show /65

傣族孔雀舞 /67
Dai Peacock Dance /69

别具匠心

蚕丝织造 / 73
Chinese Sericulture and Silk / 75

乌龙茶制作 / 77
Chinese Oolong Tea Making / 79

景德镇制瓷 / 81
Porcelain Making in Jingdezhen / 83

白酒酿制 / 85
Chinese *Baijiu* Distilling / 87

扬派盆景 / 89
Yangzhou *Penjing* / 91

制 扇 / 93
Fan Making / 95

烟火爆竹制作 / 97
Fireworks Making / 99

风筝制作 / 101
Kite Making / 103

传统香制作 / 105
Traditional Incense Making / 107

传统民居营造 / 109
Traditional Dwellings in Southern Fujian / 111

牛羊肉烹制 / 113
Beef and Mutton Cooking / 115

中医诊法 / 117
TCM Diagnostic Methods / 119

妙手丹青

汉字书法 / 123
Chinese Calligraphy / 125

剪　纸 / 127
Chinese Paper Cutting / 129

料　器 / 131
Beijing Glazeware / 133

景泰蓝 / 135
Jingtailan（Cloisonné） / 137

布艺老虎 / 139
Cloth Tiger / 141

面　花 / 143
Dough Modelling / 145

面　人 / 147
Dough Figurine / 149

糖　画 / 151
Sugar Painting / 153

泉州花灯 / 155
Quanzhou Festive Lanterns / 157

木版年画 / 159
Woodblock-Printed *Nianhua* / *161*

建筑彩绘 / 163
Architectural Decorative Painting / 165

维吾尔族服饰 / 167
Uyghur Dresses / 169

藏族唐卡 / 171
Tibetan Thangka / 173

中国花鸟画 / 175
Chinese Flower-And-Bird Painting / 177

中国山水画 / 179
Chinese Landscape Painting / 181

中国人物画 / 183
Chinese Figure Painting / 185

精雕细琢

中国篆刻 / 189
Chinese Seal Engraving / 191

雕版印刷 / 193
Woodblock Printing / 195

京 绣 / 197
Beijing Embroidery / 199

苗 绣 / 201
Miao Embroidery / 203

苏 绣 / 205
Suzhou Embroidery / 207

挑 花 / 209
Chinese Cross Stitch / 211

北京玉雕 / 213
Beijing Jade Carving / 215

石 雕 / 217
Stone Carving / 219

贝 雕 / 221
Shell Carving / 223

竹 刻 / 225
Bamboo Carving / 227

泉州木雕 / 229
Quanzhou Wood Carving / 231

泥 塑 / 233
Clay Figurines / 235

安溪竹藤编 / 237
Anxi Bamboo and Rattan Weaving / 239

香 包 / 241
Chinese Sachets / 243

北京绢花 / 245
Beijing Silk Flowers / 247

后 记 / 248

古 琴

扫码观看视频

古琴是中国最古老的弹拨乐器，
比钢琴早了几千年。
在漫长的历史岁月中，
悠远的古琴曲承载着中国的礼乐精神，
寄托着中华文人的思想与情操。
相传，古琴创始于史前传说时代的
伏羲氏和神农氏时期，
距今已有三千多年，
古琴的形制在汉代逐渐发展完备。

古琴有着丰富的文化内涵，
各部分构件都被赋予美好的寓意。
比如，
琴头长三尺六寸五分，
象征一年三百六十五天；
琴头宽六寸，
象征东南西北，苍天厚土；
琴尾四寸，
象征四季交替，生生不息。
古琴的十三个徽位代表十二月与闰月，
发挥着标记音位的作用。

古琴的音色将乐曲简化、延长，
在听觉上留下了大量的空白，
借听者的想象，
在琴音与留白之间产生流动感。
小到风花雪月，
大到家国天下，
古人把心中的万千思绪
通过琴弦传递出去，
余音绕梁，千年不散。

无论是古代还是现代，
古琴都代表着中国人的
生活态度和君子气节，
寄托着中华民族对国泰民安、
天下大同的理想追求。

让我们泡一杯花茶，
听一首琴曲，
感受穿越千年的音律
和古代圣贤的琴音心声，
获得身心的自由与伸展。

补注·延伸

秦祚之后，礼乐失驭。予嗟乎琴散久矣！后之传者，妙指美声，巧以相尚。

——范仲淹（宋）
《与唐处士书》

华绘雕琢，布藻垂文。错以犀象，籍以翠绿。

余少好音声，长而玩之。以为物有盛衰，而此无变；滋味有厌，而此不倦。可以导养神气，宣和情志。处穷独而不闷者，莫近于音声也。是故复之而不足，则吟咏以肆志；吟咏之不足，则寄言以广意。然八音之器，歌舞之象，历世才士，并为之赋颂。其体制风流，莫不相袭。称其材干，则以危苦为上；赋其声音，则以悲哀为主；美其感化，则以垂涕为贵。丽则丽矣，然未尽其理也。推其所由，似原不解音声；览其旨趣，亦未达礼乐之情也。众器之中，琴德最优。故缀叙所怀，以为之赋。

——嵇康（三国时期）
《琴赋》

独坐幽篁里，弹琴复长啸。深林人不知，明月来相照。

——王维（唐）
《竹里馆》

泠泠七弦上，静听松风寒。古调虽自爱，今人多不弹。

——刘长卿（唐）
《听弹琴》

Guqin

扫码观看视频

Guqin is the oldest plucked string musical instrument in China. It has kept alive the essence of Chinese ethos as well as the longing and sentiments of Chinese literati. It is believed that the *guqin* was invented over 3,000 years ago in prehistoric times, and acquired its shape as we know it in the Han Dynasty (206 BC-220 AD).

Guqin is rich in cultural symbolism. The length of the head of the *guqin* symbolizes 365 days in a year, and its width symbolizes the land extending in all directions. The tail stands for the four seasons. Its 13 emblems, which mark phonemes, represent twelve months and the leap month.

From personal emotions to patriotic sentiments, in both ancient and modern times, *guqin* represents Chinese people's attitudes towards life and their national traits as well as their pursuit of peace, prosperity and harmony.

Drink a cup of tea, listen to the old *guqin* melody created by ancient saints, and you will feel thoroughly relaxed and achieve perfect peace of mind.

太极拳

太极拳

扫码观看视频

飞檐走壁，飞沙走石，
天下武功，唯快不破。
可在中国有一种"太极拳"，
偏偏像是开了慢动作。

太极拳讲究以静制动，顺势而为。
注重意念的修炼，
动作柔和、轻灵，
一招一式都是动与静、虚与实的结合。
站桩，积累松沉之内力，
推手，外现刚柔之气劲。
时常练习还有修身养性、强身健体的效果。

太极拳历史悠久，有着丰厚的文化底蕴。
拳为骨，道为心。
据古书记载，
"太"的意思是大，
"极"的意思是开始和顶点。
"太极"就是产生万物的至高本源。

拳术和太极说的结合，
逐步形成了太极拳术。
民间流传着无数关于太极拳的传说故事。
在金庸先生的《倚天屠龙记》中，
太极大师张三丰在传授武艺时，
告诫徒儿不需拘泥于招式，
只要细细领会其中内涵，
看似随意出击，
实则自成章法，
无招胜有招，
体现的是中国的武术哲学。

太极拳追求的是人与自然的高度协调。
一推一进之间，
是从容恬淡的气韵风度；
一招一式之下，
是生生不息的人生体悟。
让我们跟着太极师傅一起，
放松身心，气沉丹田，
感受太极拳的魅力吧。

补注·延伸

可以御侮，可以卫生，愿以此有百利而无一害之国粹，为四百兆同胞之典型。

——蔡元培

《为〈太极拳体用全书〉题词》

太极者，无极而生，动静之机，阴阳之母。动之则分，静之则合。

——王宗岳（明）

《太极拳谱》

须要从人，不要由己；从人则活，由己则滞。

——武禹襄（清）

《打手要言》

无极而太极，太极动而生阳，动极而静，静而生阴，静极复动，一动一静，互为其根。

——周敦颐（宋）

《太极图说》

言次每以国民积弱受异族侵凌为耻，抱发扬国术振我民族尚武精神之志……要皆以锻炼体魄制敌御侮为主旨，然欲求其固精神培元气，则首推武当之太极拳一术，以其柔内蓄刚不伤元气。我民族尚武精神实利赖之。

——杨森

《太极蕴真序》

Tai Chi Quan

扫码观看视频

Leaping over rooftops and walking up walls. Swiftness is the key to all but one martial art— Tai Chi Quan, which seems to slow every motion down.

Focusing on mind-cultivation, Tai Chi Quan seeks to take the quiet approach and seize the momentum. The soft and light moves combine movement with stillness, imagination with reality. Stand still to accumulate internal force; and push hands to exude soft-firm strength. Regular practice also helps with mind and body building.

Tai Chi Quan has a long history and rich cultural heritage. According to the ancient book, "Tai" means great, and "Chi" means the beginning and apex. "Tai Chi" is the primary source of all things. The combination of boxing and Tai Chi theory gradually formed Tai Chi Quan.

There are countless legends and folklores about Tai Chi Quan in China. In one popular Martial Arts fiction, Tai Chi master Zhang Sanfeng told his disciples not to stick to the moves. "As long as you understand the essence," he said, "a random attack could be self-contained." Winning with no fixed moves embodies the philosophy of Chinese Martial Arts.

Tai Chi Quan pursues the great harmony between man and nature. Each push or pull exhibits a calm and tranquil air; and each move or style is an endless life experience. Let's follow the Tai Chi master to relax our mind and body, and feel the charm of Tai Chi Quan.

京 剧

扫码观看视频

百年戏楼,雕梁画栋。
京剧在两百多年的发展中,
集南北音律之精华,
中国传统美学之大成,
铸就了雅俗共赏的民族艺术瑰宝,
成为享誉世界的中华国粹。

清代乾隆年间,
三庆、四喜、和春、春台,
四大徽班进京,
与来自湖北的汉调艺人合作,
融合南方剧种与京腔之长,
逐渐形成了京剧,
传遍大江南北。

京剧的表演行当
分为生、旦、净、丑四门,
略施脂粉的是"生角"和"旦角",
重施油彩的是"净行",
鼻梁上一抹白粉的
就是俗称"小花脸"的"丑角"。
各行当都有一套表演程式,
唱、念、做、打,各具特色。
传统京剧擅长表现历史题材,
既有整本的大戏,
也有大量折子戏,
剧目丰富,表演考究,
凝聚着我国传统社会的
道德精神和价值取向。

戏文演绎的家国情怀、忠孝仁义,
寄托了人们对真、善、美的追求。
从个人命运到家国兴衰,
京剧,
在岁月更迭中传递着
中华文化的独特魅力。

补注·延伸

戏曲是中华文化的瑰宝，繁荣发展戏曲事业关键在人。

——习近平总书记给中国戏曲学院师生的回信

京剧艺术是中华民族艺术的瑰宝，它兼容并蓄、广征博采，有着辉煌的历史，蕴含着民族文化的精髓。

——《文化部关于印发〈国家重点京剧院团保护和扶持规划〉的通知》

宛然巾帼，无分毫矫强。不必征歌，一颦一笑，一起一坐，描摹雌软神情，几乎化境。

——小铁笛道人（清）
《日下看花记》

蓝脸的窦尔敦盗御马，红脸的关公战长沙，黄脸的典韦，白脸的曹操，黑脸的张飞，叫喳喳……

——《唱脸谱》

Peking/Beijing Opera

扫码观看视频

With a history of over 200 years, Peking Opera, or Beijing Opera, is a colorful and spectacular performance art. Combining wonderful singing and acting with elaborate costumes and make-up, it is regarded as a cultural treasure of China.

During the reign of the Qianlong Emperor (1735-1796), the "Four Great Anhui Troupes" brought Eastern China's Anhui opera to Beijing. Then they were joined by several Hubei troupes from Central China. This combination gradually formed the most influential Peking Opera.

Peking Opera features four main types of performers. The main male and female roles are called *Sheng* and *Dan* respectively; *Jing* is a painted-face male role; whereas *Chou*, or clown, has a patch of white chalk around the nose. Performers follow the established formats of singing, reciting, acting and martial arts.

The repertoire of Peking Opera includes both traditional long plays and the condensed and excerpted versions called *zhezixi*. The plays tell stories about history as well as social and family life, reflecting China's traditional cultural values.

Expressing the aesthetic ideals of the Chinese nation, Peking Opera is a precious intangible cultural heritage of all humanity.

昆 曲

扫码观看视频

不到园林，怎知春色如许，
不听昆曲，怎知江南之美？
昆曲，
是中国戏曲艺术中的一朵幽兰
盛开在姑苏水乡，
吸引着全世界的戏曲爱好者。

六百多年前，
元末诗人顾坚以南曲为灵感，
创作了昆曲的前身——昆山腔。
经过明代魏良辅等人的创新，
集南北曲调之长的"水磨调"
得以问世。
后经几代艺术家的改良，
昆曲，终于成为一个
独特而又极具生命力的剧种，
闻名天下。

吴侬软语和着丝竹笛韵，
依字行腔，一唱三叹，
再配上贴合戏文的身段动作，
细腻婉转，引人入胜。

台上人一颦一笑、一曲一调，
将听者带入一个个动人的故事中。
昆曲中的许多剧本，
如《牡丹亭》《长生殿》《桃花扇》等，
都是我国古代戏曲文学中的不朽之作。
王侯将相、才子佳人的传奇往事，
普通人的爱恨离愁，
一幕幕在昆曲中上演。
真挚的感情超越生死、世俗，
动人的故事穿越历史、国界。

历经四百年的风风雨雨，
昆曲从历史的深处走来，
满载着中华文化的硕果。
戏里戏外的悲欢离合化入曲中，
演绎着东方美学的万种风情。

补注·延伸

传承保护京剧、昆曲。继续安排资金支持京剧、昆曲保护与传承。实施中国京剧像音像集萃计划。实施当代昆曲名家收徒传艺工程,做好优秀昆曲传统折子戏录制工作。

——国务院办公厅《关于支持戏曲传承发展的若干政策》

张謇常对我说:"中国的戏剧,尤其是昆曲,不但文学一部分有价值,传统的优秀演技,也应该把他发扬光大,这是我的意见,你们的责任了。"

——梅兰芳

Kunqu Opera

扫码观看视频

How do you know what spring is like without a walk in the garden? And how can you know the beauty of Jiangnan without listening to *Kunqu* Opera? As an "orchid" of Chinese opera art flowering in the water town of Suzhou, *Kunqu* attracts opera lovers all over the world.

More than 600 years ago, a poet named Gu Jian created the predecessor of *Kunqu*—*Kunshan Qiang* based on *Nanqu*. After innovations made by Wei Liangfu and others, a tune that absorbed the merits of both north and south tunes, called *shuimodiao*, came into being. Then it gradually developed into a unique and vigorous opera known to the world.

The soft Suzhou dialect, accompanied by string and bamboo instruments, is sung in a strictly stylized way, and matched with postures that fit in with the opera text, bringing out a delicate and fascinating performance. The emotional expressions and melodious songs of the stage performers draw the audience into every engaging story.

Many plays in *Kunqu*, such as *The Peony Pavilion*, *The Palace of Eternal Life* and *The Peach Blossom Fan*, are all-time masterpieces of ancient Chinese opera literature. The legends of kings and generals, the romantic love between literati and beauties, and the love and hate of ordinary people, are all staged in *Kunqu*. Sincere love transcends life and death, or worldly affairs, and touching stories go beyond history and nations.

After 400 years of ups and downs, *Kunqu* Opera is fully loaded with the fruits of Chinese culture. The joys and sorrows inside and outside the opera are integrated into the songs and tunes, interpreting the charms of oriental aesthetics.

皮影戏

扫码观看视频

皮影戏又称"影子戏",
一张白色的幕布后,
匠人们熟练地操纵着人偶剪影。
栩栩如生的人物在手中
上下翻飞、左右腾挪,
配合着民间乐器和各色唱腔,
精彩的故事轮番上演。

相传,皮影戏起源于汉武帝时期,
在当时是王公贵族的娱乐活动。
元代,皮影艺术在民间广泛流传的同时,
还伴随商业贸易传到了中亚地区。
到了明清时期,
皮影戏在欧洲各国风靡一时,
诗人歌德就描写过
幼年观看皮影戏的有趣经历。

皮影工艺制作考究,
兽皮经过雕刻、上色、缝缀、
涂漆等工序,
摇身一变,
就成了各色精致的角色形象。
皮影造型丰富多变、线条精巧细致,
在没有电影、电视的年代,
皮影曾陪伴许多孩子的童年时光。

中国皮影戏比电影早了两千多年。
在传承与发展中,
皮影这项古老的艺术
也迸发着新的生机。
瞧,这套以"冰雪运动"
为主题的皮影,
生动展现了跳台滑雪、
花样滑冰等活动,
传统的技艺与冬奥相结合,
光影流转,
跃动着生命与活力。

古老与现代,
传统与创新,
多少传奇故事、神话传说,
定格在一幕幕皮影戏中。

补注·延伸

三尺生绡作戏台，全凭十指逞诙谐。

——释惠明（清末民初）
《手影戏》

逢节庆日，每一坊巷口，无乐棚去处，多设小影戏棚子，以防本坊游人小儿相失，以引聚之。

——孟元老（宋）
《东京梦华录》

京师有富家子，少孤、专财，群无赖百方诱导之。而此子甚好看弄影戏，每弄至斩关羽，辄为之泣下，嘱弄者且缓之。

——张耒（宋）
《明道杂志》

凡影戏乃京师人初以素纸雕镞，后用彩色装皮为之，其话本与讲史书者颇同，大抵真假相半，公忠者雕以正貌，奸邪者与之丑貌，盖亦寓褒贬于市俗之眼戏也。

——耐得翁（宋）
《都城记胜》

Chinese Shadow Puppetry

扫码观看视频

Also known as shadow plays, Chinese Shadow Puppetry is acted with a translucent cloth screen illuminated from behind. Puppeteers manipulate the figures using rods, creating the illusion of moving images. Accompanied by music and singing, fascinating stories are told on this special stage.

The Chinese Shadow Puppetry can be traced back to the Western Han period (206BC-24AD), when it was enjoyed by the nobles.

Then in Yuan Dynasty (1206-1368), shadow plays were distributed all over China and were spread to Central Asia.

In the next few centuries, shadow puppetry reached Europe. The Europeans, including the German poet Johann Wolfgang von Goethe (1749-1832), were so impressed by shadow plays.

Most shadow puppets are made of leather. Different processes, including carving, painting, sewing and lacquering, are needed to create such colorful silhouette figures.

In the days before film and television, shadow plays were a popular entertainment, especially the youth.

Known as the oldest motion picture storytelling, this 2000-year-old ancient art is embracing new elements as well. For instance, these figures vividly depict ice and snow sports such as ski jumping and figure skating.

The Olympic Winter Games are expressed through this traditional art, which has gained new vitality in the modern world.

This art of light and shadow has reclaimed its past glory, taking on new styles to pass on legends, history and culture.

泉州南音

扫码观看视频

泉州南音是现存历史最悠久的
传统古乐,
不需时光机,
如今的我们也能享受
古人听过的美妙音乐。
几千年前,
中原的移民来到闽南地区,
带来了音乐文化,
孕育了这优美而又古老的音乐。

泉州南音起源于唐,形成于宋,
主要乐器有
"上四管"和"下四管"两种组合。
"上四管"常用琵琶和三弦,
"下四管"常用中音唢呐和扁鼓,
原汁原味地保留了中原古韵,
至今仍然延续着唐代的演奏方式。
看,这叫"横抱琵琶",
是不是和敦煌壁画中的飞天一样优雅?

南音的体系由"指""谱""曲"
三大部分构成,主题丰富,
有的歌唱四季景色、骏马奔驰,
有的演绎唐诗宋词、传奇故事,
曲调优美,委婉深情。

南音之美,也被定格在传奇书画中。
南唐顾闳中的《韩熙载夜宴图》里
就有演奏南音的场景,
画中宾客聚精会神地倾听着演奏,
嘈嘈切切错杂弹,大珠小珠落玉盘,
千年后的我们似乎也能听见。

泉州南音是"中国音乐的活化石",
名扬海外,
在东南亚等地也极受欢迎。
歌声婉转、琴瑟和鸣,
穿越千年仍延音不止,余音绕梁。

补注·延伸

风雅颂乃是乐章之腔调,如言仲吕调,大石调,越调之类。……问:"周礼大司乐说宫、商、角、征、羽与七声不合,如何?"曰:"此是降神之乐,如黄钟为宫,大吕为角,太簇为征,应钟为羽,自是四乐各举其一者而言之。以大吕为角,则南吕为宫;太簇为征,则林钟为宫;应钟为羽,则太簇为宫。以七声推之合如此……"又曰:"所谓'黄钟宫,大吕羽',这便是调。谓如头一声是宫声,尾后一声亦是宫声,这便是宫调。若是其中按拍处,那五音依旧都用,不只是全用宫。"

——朱熹(宋)

《朱子语类》

Quanzhou Nanyin

扫码观看视频

As one of the oldest existing musical forms, *Nanyin* is central to the culture of the people of Minnan in southern Fujian Province along China's southeastern coast.

Thousands of years ago, immigrants from Central China came here, bringing with them their music culture, which later developed into *Nanyin*.

The complete set of distinctive musical instruments used in *Nanyin* has been established for over 1000 years, including plucked instruments such as *Pipa* and *Sanxian*, as well as midrange *Suona* and drums.

Nanyin performance today is the same as that in Tang Dynasty (618-907).

For instance, the *Pipa* is played horizontally, just like the elegant Flying Apsaras painted in the Dunhuang Grottoes.

Nanyin comprises three forms: instrumental, instrumental with vocals, and ballads accompanied by an ensemble. Some of them capture the beauty of the natural world; whereas others preserve ancient poems and folklore.

Nanyin performances were depicted in ancient Chinese paintings. For instance, in the 1000-year-old painting which vividly represents an evening banquet hosted by the Southern Tang Minister Han Xizai, the host and guests were listening to the *Nanyin* music. Like "pearls tumbling onto a jade tray", the unique and delicate tonality of the *Pipa* has been appreciated by the Chinese people for thousands of years.

Spreading from its birthplace Quanzhou, *Nanyin* has become well-received overseas, especially in Southeast Asia.

In 2009, it was inscribed on the UNESCO's Representative List of the Intangible Cultural Heritage of Humanity.

围 棋

扫码观看视频

黑白论道,围地攻防你来我往;
落子无悔,进退之间谁为先手。
围棋,
诞生于四千多年前的中国,
既是一种艺术,
又包含着中华古典哲学。

围棋结构简单,却蕴含着
深刻的奥义与丰富的文化内涵。
棋盘四方,
由上古文明《河图》演变而来,
象征宇宙洪荒;
棋子为圆,一黑一白,
寓意阴阳互化,博弈间此消彼长;
棋盘之上19条线纵横经纬,
形成361个交点,
象征农历361天;
9个圆点称作"星",
中央星位唤为"天元"。
方圆中包罗万象,

将天、地、人融为一体。
驰骋于棋盘上,
就是在天人合一的境界中
感悟人生的哲理。

古往今来,
无数"棋手"穷其一生
只为围棋一事。
近代"棋圣"吴清源自幼学习围棋,
直至晚年,
仍致力于围棋研究,
提出"六合之棋",
将围棋的大局观置于高地,
追求整体的平衡与中和。

棋盘如同一面镜子,
投射出棋手心念的流动。
人生如棋,棋如人生。
一步一子,指引心之所向。

补注·延伸

棋盘为地子为天，色按阴阳造化全。下到玄微通变处，笑夸当日烂柯仙。

——《西游记》

棋之道在乎恬默，而取舍为急。仁则能全，义则能守，礼则能变，智则能兼，信则能克。君子知斯五者，庶几可以言棋矣。

——潘慎修（宋）
《棋说》

三百六十，以象周天之数，分为四隅，以象四时，隅各九十路，以象其日，外周七十二路，以象其候。

——《棋经十三篇》

略观围棋兮，法于用兵。三尺之局兮，为战斗场。陈聚士卒兮，两敌相当。拙者无功兮，弱者先亡。自有中和兮，请说其方。

——马融（汉）
《围棋赋》

The Game of Go

扫码观看视频

The game of Go was created in China over 4,000 years ago. It is not only an art, but contains Chinese classical philosophy.

The square Go board evolved from the ancient "River Map", which symbolizes the prehistoric universe. The round "stones" are black or white, implying the mutual transformation of yin and yang, with unity in opposition. The 19×19 grid of lines contain 361 points, representing the 361 days of the Chinese lunar calendar. The 9 major dots are called "star points", and the one at board center is called "tianyuan". The board and stones are all-encompassing, integrating the sky, the earth and the people. Competing on the board is to realize the philosophy of harmony between human and nature.

Throughout history, countless Go masters have devoted their lives to this game. The "Sage of Go" in the 20th century, Wu Qingyuan learned to play Go since childhood. He concentrated on the study of Go until his later years, and proposed the idea of "Liuhe Go (the unity of six dimensions)". He valued the big picture in the game of Go, and pursued an overall balance and harmony.

The Go board is like a mirror, reflecting the flow of the players' thoughts. Life is like Go, and Go is like life, one step at a time, guiding the direction of the heart.

象　棋

扫码观看视频

马路边、公园里，小方桌上下象棋，
这是很多中国孩子的童年记忆。
象棋在中国
有着上千年的历史和丰厚的思想内涵，
融合了
道家思想、儒家思想和军事思想，
并吸收了多种智慧。

两方在方形格状棋盘上进行对弈。
由执红棋的一方先走，
双方轮流各走一招，
马走"日"字，
象走"田"字，
车走直路，士走斜线，
谁先把对方的首领（将、帅）"将死"，
谁就获胜。

象棋模拟了古代战争，
棋盘中间的分界线"楚河汉界"
便是由真实的历史演变而来。
秦末，楚汉相争，
以楚河为界中分天下，
向西是汉，向东是楚。
象棋再现了当年两大王朝
争夺天下的历史故事。

古往今来，
象棋以独特的博弈方式、
鲜明的竞技特点，
在中华传统文化中占据了一席之地。
象棋也是怡神益智的活动，
对提高思维能力、陶冶情操
有着积极的作用。
让我们以棋会友，
感受中国象棋文化。

补注·延伸

下棋不能无争,争的范围有大有小,有斤斤计较而因小失大者,有不拘小节而眼观全局者,有短兵相接,作生死斗者,有各自为战而旗鼓相当者,有赶尽杀绝一步不让者,有好勇斗狠同归于尽者,有一面下棋一面诮骂者,但最不幸的是争的范围超出了棋盘,而拳足交加。

——梁实秋
《下棋》

蓖蔽象棋,有六簿些。分曹并进,遒相迫些。成枭而牟,呼五白些。

——屈原(战国时期)
《楚辞·招魂》

何处逢神仙,传此棋上旨。静持生杀权,密照安危理。接胜如云舒,御敌如山止。突围秦师震,诸侯皆披靡。入险汉斜危,奇兵翻背水。势应不可隳,关河常表里。南轩春日长,国手相得喜。泰山不碍目,疾雷不经耳。一子贵千金,一路重千里。精思入于神。变化胡能拟。成败系之人,吾当著棋史。

——范仲淹(宋)
《赠棋者》

小艺无难精,上智有未解。君看橘中戏,妙不出局外。屹然两国立,限以大河界。连营凛中权,四壁设坚械。三十二子者,一一具变态。先登如挑敌,分布如备塞。

——刘克庄(宋)
《象弈一首呈叶潜仲》

Xiangqi/the Chinese Chess

扫码观看视频

Playing chess on the small square table by the roadside or in the park is the childhood memory of many Chinese people.

Xiangqi, or the Chinese chess, has a history of over a thousand years. It combined Taoism, Confucianism and military thoughts.

Two sides play on a square grid chessboard. The red one generally moves first, then the two sides take turns.

There are 32 pieces of Chinese chess. Different pieces should take different paths. Whoever checkmates the other's general first wins.

The Chinese chess simulates ancient warfare. The name of the "boundary" of the two sides comes from the history.

At the end of the Qin Dynasty (221BC-207BC), the River Chu was the boundary between the two warring states, with Han to the west and Chu to the east. *Xiangqi* recreates the famous war in the Chinese history.

Throughout history, *Xiangqi* occupies a significant place in the traditional Chinese culture, with its unique game style and distinctive competitive charm.

Xiangqi is also a refreshing and educational activity, which has a positive effect on mind and spirit building. Let's meet our friends at the chessboard and feel the charm of Chinese chess.

龙　舞

扫码观看视频

你见过龙吗？
见过龙飞舞吗？
来了，
这是龙舞传承人在庙会上的表演现场。

听人说，
中国人在三千年前就开始舞龙了，
那时是为了祈求天上的神仙
保佑人间风调雨顺，
保佑农民有个好收成。
现在，舞龙已经成了
一种民间的节日风俗。
把长龙舞起来，
可以烘托节日喜庆、祥和的
热烈气氛。
龙舞在中国各地的节庆中
都可以见到，
各地的龙风格多样。
传统的龙头、龙身和龙尾
通常由竹篾扎成，
一节一节地用绸子连起来，
再用颜料画出龙的鳞片。
龙头、龙身都有木把，
人们握着木把，
就可以让龙腾飞起来。

舞龙好看在哪儿？
龙头带动龙身跑，
还要舞出花儿来。
"翻滚""绞缠""穿插""窜跃"
都少不了。

龙舞，集合了中华传统武术、
曲艺和舞蹈的动作，
也是一种体育活动。
龙是中华民族的图腾，
象征着人们对美好生活的向往。

解码中华文化基因

补注·延伸

上元张灯火，自初八九至十五日，辉煌达旦，并扮演龙灯、狮灯及其他杂剧，喧阗街市，有月逐人、尘随马之观。

——《铜梁县志·风俗篇》

龙舞，舞龙者一人为头，后为龙尾，次一人直手抱前者脚夹后者，挨次第抬向街直走，则念曰：骑龙头龙头落下水，骑龙尾龙尾竖上天。

——《海康县续志·风俗》

奉牲祷，以甲乙日为大苍龙一，长八丈，居中央。为小龙七，各长四丈，于东方，皆东乡，其间相去八尺。小童八人，皆斋三日，服青衣而舞之，田啬夫亦斋三日，服青衣而立之。

——董仲舒（汉）
《春秋繁露·求雨》

龙生于水，被五色而游，故神。欲小则化如蚕蠋，欲大则藏于天下；欲尚则凌于云气，欲下则入千深泉。

——《管子·水地篇》

黄龙入藏生黄泉。黄泉之埃，上为黄云，阴阳相薄为雷，激扬为电……青龙入藏生青泉。青泉之埃，上为青云，阴阳相薄为雷，激扬为电。

——刘安（汉）
《淮南子·地形训》

Dragon Dance

扫码观看视频

Chinese dragon is a majestic beast associated with heavenly beneficence. Dragon dances have been indispensable to Chinese festivals and events.

Originating about 3000 years ago, dragon dance was a type of rain rituals which involved a dragon image animated by dancers to secure favorable weather and a good harvest.

Nowadays, dragon dance has become a folk custom during holidays. A flying dragon can create such a festive atmosphere.

Appearing in celebrations all over China, the dancing dragons vary in styles. Traditionally, different sections of the dragon, including the head, body, and tail, are constructed of bamboo hoops and covered with silk fabric, on which dragon scales are painted. Both the head and the body have supporting poles, which are used to manipulate the dragon.

How to appreciate the dragon dance? Various dragon dance techniques bring the dragon to life, including "roaming" "entangling" "crossing" and "jumping". Dragon dance combines the Chinese martial arts, folk music and dance movements.

Flying the dragon, which is the totem of the Chinese nation, symbolizes Chinese people's yearning for a more beautiful life.

狮 舞

扫码观看视频

看！闹市区里有狮子！
小场面，来中国过个春节你就知道了。
狮舞是中国民间的传统表演艺术，
融合了武术、民乐和舞蹈等
多种元素。

最常见的狮舞由两个人配合，
一人演头，一人演尾，
踩着鼓点，像小狮子一样，
"眨眼""舔身""抖毛""吐球"，
憨态可掬，栩栩如生。

狮子是中国人心中的瑞兽，
能够驱灾辟邪，求吉纳福。
远古时期，
村子里总有野猪闯来糟蹋庄稼、
咬伤儿童，
人们就在干活的时候
扮作狮子吓跑它们，
这就是狮舞的由来。

狮舞分为南狮和北狮。
南狮技巧高超，矫健凶猛，
在表演之前会举行"点睛"仪式，
把朱砂涂在狮子的眼睛上，
象征给予生命。
每逢节庆，必有南狮助兴，
寓意着驱邪避灾，添瑞纳福。

北狮灵动活泼，娇憨可爱，
经常成对出现，
有时还会带上一只小狮子，
寓意家庭美满，尽享天伦。

别看狮舞跳起来如此轻盈，
真想舞好，
可是需要长年累月的练习呢！
台上一分钟，台下十年功，
这就是名副其实的"中国功夫"。

补注·延伸

戏有五方狮子,高丈余,各衣五色,每一狮子,有十二人,戴红抹额,衣画衣,执红拂子,谓之狮子郎,舞太平乐曲。

——段安节(唐)
《乐府杂录》

西凉伎,西凉伎,假面胡人假狮子。刻木为头丝作尾,金镀眼睛银帖齿。奋迅毛衣摆双耳,如从流沙来万里。

——白居易(唐)
《西凉伎》

方相氏掌蒙熊皮,黄金四目,玄衣朱裳,执戈扬盾,帅百隶而时傩,以索室驱疫。

——《周礼·夏官》

Lion Dance

扫码观看视频

Look! Lions in the downtown area! Don't fuss. Why not come to China at the Spring Festival? Lion dance is a traditional Chinese performing art, combining martial arts, folk music and dance. Lion dance consists of two people. One plays the head and the other the tail. They dance like a little lion which can blink, lick its body, shake hair and spit ball, cute and lifelike.

The lion is an auspicious beast in China, able to exorcise evil and seek blessing. In ancient times, when wild boars came to the village, destroyed crops and bit children, people would pretend to be lions to scare them away. This is the origin of lion dance.

There are two types of lion dances (Southern Style and Northern Style). The southern-style lions are highly skilled, athletic and fierce. An "eye painting" ceremony is held before the performance. Applying cinnabar on its eyes means giving life to the lion. During festivals, the lion dance is performed to celebrate, which means to drive away evil and to bring good fortune. The northern-style lions are agile, lively and cute. They often appear in pairs, sometimes also bring a little lion, symbolizing a happy family.

The dancing lions are so light-footed, but it takes years and months of practice. "One minute on stage, ten years' work off stage." This is also "Chinese kung fu".

口 技

扫码观看视频

口技是一种中国民间的表演技艺，
主要运用人体的
口、齿、唇、舌、喉等部位，
以独特的运气和发声方法，
模仿风雨雷电、动物鸣叫、乐器等
自然界和生活中的各种声音。

口技的起源可以追溯到上古时期，
那时人们为了狩猎，
经常模仿动物的叫声引诱猎物。

宋代，
口技表演趋于成熟，
表演者隐身在一块屏障后面，
一人便可模仿市井中的各色声响：
狗叫、小孩啼哭等，
惟妙惟肖。

清代有一位人称"百鸟张"的
口技表演者，
十分擅长模仿禽类鸣叫，
他的表演甚至可以吸引
鸟群来寻找同伴。

近现代，
口技以话筒等音响设备辅助，
可以模仿电波、飞机、大炮的声音，
开辟出全新的声音领域。
怎么样，是不是很神奇？
快来一起学学中国的口技吧！

补注·延伸

围设青绫好隐身，象声一一妙于真。谁知众口空嘈杂，绝技曾无第二人。

——李声振（清）

《百戏竹枝词》

京中有善口技者。会宾客大宴，于厅事之东北角，施八尺屏障，口技人坐屏障中，一桌、一椅、一扇、一抚尺而已。众宾团坐。少顷，但闻屏障中抚尺一下，满坐寂然，无敢哗者。

——林嗣环（清）

《口技》

Oral Stunts

扫码观看视频

Kouji is a type of Chinese folk performing art. Performers mainly use mouth, teeth, lips, tongue, and throat with unique breathing patterns and vocalization to imitate wind, rainfall, thunder, musical instruments, animal call and other sounds in nature and human life.

Chinese oral stunts can date back to ancient times, when people often imitated the sound of animals to lure the prey for hunting. In the Song Dynasty (960-1279), oral stunt performance became mature. The performer would hide behind a screen and vividly imitate various sounds in daily life by himself, such as dogs' bark and children' cry.

In the Qing Dynasty (1644-1911), a *kouji* performer known as "Hundred-Bird Zhang" was very good at imitating different bird chirps. His performance could even attract birds to "look for their fellow".

Modern oral stunts are assisted by audio equipment such as microphone. They can imitate the sounds of radio wave, cannon and plane, which breaks new ground for vocal imitation. Isn't it amazing? Let's learn Chinese oral stunts together!

高　跷

扫码观看视频

看！迎面走来个三米高的巨人！
这是中国传统民俗活动——踩高跷。

表演者脚踩在细长的木棍上，
腿和木棍用绳子绑在一起，
服饰多模仿戏曲行头，
常用道具有扇子、手绢、木棍、刀枪等。

传统高跷分为"文""武"两类，
"文跷"侧重故事情节，
"武跷"侧重动作设计。

踩跷者时常扮成
传统民间故事里的人物，
可以是《西游记》里的齐天大圣孙悟空，
也可以是《三国演义》里
骁勇善战的关二爷。

高跷在中国起源很早，
先秦时期就已经十分流行。
据民间传说，
高跷这种形式原来是古代人
为了采集树上的野果为食，
给自己腿上绑上两根长棍，
后来逐渐发展成
中国传统节日期间的民俗活动。

在锣鼓乐队的伴奏声中，
表演者们踩着高跷走街串巷，
人们追随表演队伍，
争相观看，挤满了街道。
大人小孩都十分兴奋，
好不热闹！

踩高跷是一门技术活，
初学者往往容易摔跤。
欢迎大家来中国，
体验一下这流传千年的民俗活动吧。

补注·延伸

宋有兰子者,以枝干宋元。宋元台而使见其枝。以双枝长信其身,属其胫,并趋并驰,并七剑迭而跃之,五剑常在空中,元君大惊,立赐金帛。

——《列子·说符》

捷足居然逐队高,步虚应许快联曹。笑他立脚无根据,也在人间走一遭。

——恩竹樵(清)

《咏秧歌》

Stilts

扫码观看视频

Look! A three-meter-tall giant is approaching! This is a traditional Chinese folk activity—walking on stilts.

The performers step on wooden poles, their calves and poles tied together with ropes. They wear costumes from opera characters, with props like fans, handkerchiefs, sticks, broadswords and spears in hand.

The performance can be divided into *wenqiao* and *wuqiao*. While *wenqiao* stresses appearance and amusement, *wuqiao* emphasizes action and movement. Stilters often act as characters in traditional folk tales—either the omnipotent Monkey King in *Journey to the West*, or the fighting god Guan Yu in *Romance of the Three Kingdoms*.

Stilts originated very early in China, and were very popular during the Pre-Qin Period（before 221BC）. According to the folk tale, the ancient Chinese began using stilts to help them gather fruits from trees. This practical use of stilts gradually developed into a kind of folk dance during traditional Chinese festivals.

Performers walk on stilts to the music of gong and drum. People follow the performers and swarm into the streets, eager to watch the performance. Old or young, everyone is so excited.

Walking on stilts requires high skill, and beginners fall easily. But practice makes perfect. If you're confident enough, come to China and give this thousand-year-old folk activity a try.

秧 歌

扫码观看视频

秧歌是中国北方农村广泛流行的
民间舞蹈，
不需搭台，观众也无须落座。
根据不同的表演风格，
秧歌又分为高跷秧歌和地秧歌。

秧歌孕育在乡土，流传于民间，
在中国已有千年历史。
清代吴锡麟《新年杂咏抄》载：
"秧歌，南宋灯宵之村田乐也。"
农民在插秧、拔草时，
为了减轻劳作之苦，
便哼起了歌，
身体随性扭动，
再融入独特步伐，
就形成了多姿多彩的秧歌舞。

人们扭秧歌时会穿上色彩艳丽的服装，
手里拿着伞或手绢等道具，
在锣鼓、唢呐等乐器的伴奏下
尽情舞蹈。
不同地域的舞法各不相同，
东北秧歌威武雄浑，
加入了骑马、狩猎等动作；
陕北秧歌淳朴自然，
步伐平稳，队形变化丰富。
秧歌舞队少则数十人，多达上百人，
是农民闲暇时不可缺少的娱乐活动。

每逢春节、元宵等传统节日，
人们便扭起秧歌来庆祝，
比歌赛舞，好不热闹！
感兴趣的话，
你也来学一学，扭一扭吧！

解码中华文化基因

补注·延伸

春波夜涨韩江水，绕郭秧歌雨中起。

——丘逢甲（清）
《喜雨词》

孤村隐隐起微烟，处处秧歌竞插田。

——苏曼殊
《淀江道中口占》

笙鼓水龙喧社处，儿童竹马跃城阴。

——孔天胤（明）
《谢郡侯张公祷雨辄应》

立春先一日，官府率士民，具春牛芒神，迎春于东郊。里人行户装渔、樵、耕、读，伶人为角抵诸戏剧，充十二行，各执事前导。结彩为楼，城关乡镇老幼男女皆聚观焉。至立春日，官吏各执彩杖，击土牛者三，谓之鞭春，以示劝农意，造小春牛送缙绅家，谓送春。

——《汾阳县志》

Yangko Dance (Sidling Songs)

扫码观看视频

Yangko is a popular folk dance in rural northern China, which does not require any stage or audience seats. According to its performance styles, the *yangko* dance can be subdivided into stilt *yangko* and ground *yangko*.

Born in the countryside and spread among people, *yangko* has a thousand-year history in China.

According to the record [*Copies of New Year's Miscellaneous Chants*, Wu Xilin, The Qing Dynasty (1644-1911)], *yangko* is the rural music performed at the Lantern Festival in Southern Song Dynasty (1127-1279). When transplanting rice seedlings, farmers chanted songs and twisted their bodies to relieve the pain of labor. Later, unique dance moves were added to the chants, giving birth to various *yangko* dances.

When twisting *yangko* dance, people will wear colorful costumes, hold umbrellas or handkerchiefs in their hands, and dance to the music of gongs, drums and suonas.

The dance moves vary from region to region. The Northeast *yangko* is powerful and mighty, with movements imitating horse-riding and hunting, while the Northern Shaanxi *yangko* is simple and natural, with steady steps and rich formation changes. A *yangko* dance team can have dozens or hundreds of people. *Yangko* is an indispensable leisure-time entertainment for farmers.

During traditional festivals like the Spring Festival and the Lantern Festival, Chinese people will twist *yangko* as celebrations and competitions.

If you are interested, come to learn how to "twist *yanko*"!

抖空竹

扫码观看视频

你见过抖空竹吗?
空竹,又称响葫芦,
是一种民间传统玩具。
人们抖动线绳使空竹高速旋转,
发出嗡嗡的响声。
听,又有人在抖空竹啦!

过去空竹多用竹、木制作,
现在大多是塑料材质,
小小空竹可有着超过
六百年的流行历史呢!
上至王宫贵族,下至平民百姓
都喜欢没事"抖一抖"。

空竹为圆盘状,中有木轴,
分单轮和双轮两种。
抖空竹上手并不难,

把棉绳两头系在抖竿上,
再把棉绳绕空竹轴一两圈,
练习几回,就能把空竹抖起来了。
别看它简单,想要精通可不容易,
绕、摆、旋、绷、抄、抛
是抖空竹的基本六字诀,
其他技巧花样还有上百种,
真正的大师,
能把空竹抖得精彩绝伦,令人眼花缭乱。

抖空竹传承至今,仍深受大众喜爱,
已经成为一项全民体育活动。
在中国的公园、广场,
有许多精通抖空竹的人。
试着加入他们,
你也能掌握这项酷炫的技术!

补注·延伸

两头以竹简为之,中贯以柱,以绳拉之作声。唯京师之空钟,其形圆而扁,加一轴,贯两轮,其音较外省所制,清越而长。

——梁溪坐关老人(清)
《清代野记》

空钟者,形如车轮,中有短轴,儿童以双杖系棉线拨弄之,俨如天外神钟。

——富察敦崇(清)
《燕京岁时记》

空钟者,刳木中空,旁口,荡以沥青,卓地如仰钟,而柄其上之平。别一绳绕其柄,别一竹尺有孔,度其绳而抵格空钟,绳勒右却,竹勒左却。一勒,空钟轰而疾转,大者声钟,小亦蛞蜣飞声,一钟声歇时乃已,制径寸至八九寸,其放之,一人至三人。

——刘侗(明)、于奕正(明)
《帝京景物略·春场》

杨柳抽青复陨黄,儿童镇日聚如狂。空钟放罢寒冬近,又见围喧踢毽场。

——前因居士(清)
《日下新讴》

京师儿童,有抖空钟之戏,截竹为二短筒,中作小榦,连而不断,实其两头,窍其中间,以绳绕其小榦,引两头擞抖之,声如洪钟,甚为可听。

——《燕京杂记》

杨柳儿活,抽陀螺;杨柳儿青,放空钟;杨柳儿死,踢毽子;杨柳发芽,打拔儿。

——《明代小儿戏具谣》

Diabolo Playing

扫码观看视频

Have you seen people playing diabolo? Also known as ringing calabash, diabolo is a traditional Chinese folk toy. People shake the string to make diabolo rotate at a high speed, which creates a buzzing sound. Listen, someone is playing diabolo!

Diabolo used to be made of bamboo and wood, but now it is mostly made of plastic. Diabolo has a long history of more than 600 years in China, and it was popular with people of all ages, both royal families and common folks.

Diabolo is disc-shaped and has a wooden shaft in it. There are two kinds of diabolo, one with one wheel and the other with double wheels. Playing diabolo is not difficult to learn. Tie both ends of a cotton rope to the shaking rod, wrap the cotton rope around the diabolo shaft one or two times and practice several times to shake diabolo. But it is not easy to be a good diabolo player. Winding, swinging, spinning, stretching, lifting and tossing are the six basic ways of playing diabolo, which can develop into over a hundred complex ways of playing the toy. One who is good at it can play diabolo with dazzling skills and leave spectators deeply impressed.

Today diabolo playing is popular across the country. In China's parks and wide open spaces, one can see many people playing diabolo with mastery. Join them and master this cool stunt!

传统箭术

扫码观看视频

看那个人,
眼神专注,挽弓搭箭,英气逼人。
这就是咱们乐都群众的
主要健身运动——传统箭术。

传统箭术又名南山射箭,
最早可以追溯到明朝中期。
当时的藏族人民大多习练骑射技艺,
形成了独特的箭术文化。
后来,受到藏族影响,
聚居的其他民族
也渐渐喜欢上了这项运动。
射箭不仅能强身健体,
还能给习射者带来精神上的愉悦,
历史上一度形成了
"人人能射,户户备弓"的风气。

每到夏季,乐都南山地区的各乡镇
都会举办射箭比赛,
比赛以村为单位,实行主客场赛制。

箭手们身着民族服装,
个个气宇轩昂,
驾着骏马,拉紧弓弦。
"嗖"的一下,
在空中划出一道有力的弧线,
直中靶心,
引得观众欢呼一片。
南山射箭大赛
同时也是"花儿会"和物资交流会。
到了比赛这天,各路商贩云集,
观众在赛场边唱着传统歌曲
"花儿"和"拉伊",
好不热闹!

一张弓,一支箭,
射出了如虹的气势,
也把各个民族的心串联在一起。
快和着歌声,跟上"南山箭客"的骏马,
一起来围观这场骑射盛宴吧!

补注·延伸

君子无所争,必也射乎!揖让而升,下而饮,其争也君子。

——孔子(春秋时期)

《论语》

射者,仁之道也。射求正诸己,己正而后发。发而不中,则不怨胜己者,反求诸己而已矣。

——戴圣(汉)

《礼记》

宿昔秉良弓,楛矢何参差。控弦破左的,右发摧月支。

——曹植(三国时期)

《白马篇》

老夫聊发少年狂,左牵黄,右擎苍,锦帽貂裘,千骑卷平冈。为报倾城随太守,亲射虎,看孙郎。

酒酣胸胆尚开张。鬓微霜,又何妨!持节云中,何日遣冯唐?会挽雕弓如满月,西北望,射天狼。

——苏轼(宋)

《江城子·密州出猎》

Traditional Archery

扫码观看视频

Look at that girl who concentrates on the bow and arrow. This is traditional archery, a major sport for people in Ledu, which is located in Northwest China.

Traditional archery, also known as Nanshan Archery, dates back to the 16th century. To resist the intrusion of surrounding tribes, most Tibetan people practiced horse-riding and archery. Later, influenced by Tibetan people, other ethnic groups also came to love this sport. Archery can not only strengthen the body, but also bring spiritual pleasure. There once was a trend that "everyone can shoot, and every household has a bow".

Each summer, all the towns and villages in the Nanshan area of Ledu will hold archery competition. The archers, dressed in traditional costume, look dignified on their horses, pull their bowstrings tight and draw a powerful arc in the air. The arrow hits the bullseye and gets cheers from the audience. Nanshan archery competition is also a commodity fair. On the day of the competition, many vendors gather from different places, and the audience sing traditional songs around the competition field.

The archery connects people of all ethnic groups. Let's keep up with the horses of "Nanshan Archers" in the singing, and watch this great competition of horse-riding and arrow-shooting.

提线木偶戏

扫码观看视频

提线木偶戏古称悬丝傀儡，
闽南俗称嘉礼，又名线戏，
是一门古老的汉族艺术。
木偶戏演起来，可比真人演难多了。
除了每个角色都有个性化的
服饰与妆发外，
还要配合角色性格
设计表演一整套动作，
这繁复的动作都要靠操控提线来完成。

木偶戏起源于秦汉时期，
在古代，人们相信木偶可以与神灵对话，
每逢婚丧嫁娶或者大型庆典，
艺人们都会奉上一出精彩的木偶表演，
向神灵传达人们的心愿。

艺人在表演木偶戏时必须"一心多用"，
以独特的"傀儡调"唱出台词，
同时每根手指控制 1 到 3 根提线，
以实现各种舞蹈姿势和武打动作。

大型提线木偶剧《赵氏孤儿》，
取材于我国古典四大悲剧，
在表演过程中实现了碾药、
拔剑、连续甩发等高难度动作，
成功地用木头人演绎出一段
感人肺腑的传奇故事。

泉州提线木偶戏
至今仍保留了七百多出传统剧目，
当你"片荒"的时候，
不妨来看看这些精彩绝伦的木偶戏吧！

补注·延伸

自昔传云："起于汉祖,在平城,为冒顿所围,其城一面即冒顿妻阏氏,兵强于三面。垒中绝食。陈平访知阏氏妒忌,即造木偶人,运机关,舞于郫间。阏氏望见,谓是生人,虑下其城,冒顿必纳妓女,遂退军。"……后乐家翻为戏。

——段安节(唐)
《乐府杂录·傀儡子》

刻木牵丝作老翁,鸡皮鹤发与真同。须臾弄罢寂无事,还似人生一梦中。

——唐玄宗
《吟傀儡》

窟儡子,亦曰魁儡子,作偶人以戏,善歌舞,本丧家之乐也,汉末始用之于嘉会……今闾市盛行焉。

——杜佑(唐)
《通典》

每将过郡县,先令倡卒弄傀儡以观人情,虑其邀击。

——《旧唐书》

Quanzhou String Puppet Show

扫码观看视频

The string puppet show is called Jiali in South Fujian dialect. It is an old Han art performed at the city of Quanzhou.

To act with puppets is more difficult than with real persons. Besides personalized costumes and make-up for each character, a whole set of actions in line with the character's personality must be designed and carried out by pulling the strings.

The puppet show originated about 2,000 years ago. Ancient people believed puppets could talk to gods. So, at weddings, funerals, or big celebrations, performers would stage a puppet show to convey people's wishes to gods.

When doing the shows, the performers have to "multitask"—singing the character's lines in a unique "puppet tune", while manipulating 1 to 3 strings with each finger, to achieve various dance poses and martial arts actions.

The puppet show *The Orphan of Zhao* is based on one major Chinese classical tragedy. Difficult moves like grinding medicine, drawing swords, spinning hair were integrated into the show, bringing a touching legend to life.

More than 700 traditional plays are preserved in the showlist of Quanzhou String Puppet Show. Next time when you run out of shows to watch, take a look at these wonderful puppet shows!

傣族孔雀舞

扫码观看视频

在中国的民族舞中，
有一种以孔雀为创作灵感的舞蹈
——傣族孔雀舞。
生活在云南的傣族人民能歌善舞，
把孔雀视为象征吉祥的"圣鸟"，
傣族孔雀舞是当地最负盛名的舞种。

相传在数千年前，
傣族祖先模仿孔雀的姿态，
创造出了这种优美的舞蹈。
东汉时，
使者将孔雀舞传到了洛阳。
经过数代舞者的传承与发展，
形成了流传至今的傣族孔雀舞。

傣族孔雀舞以独舞为主，也有双人舞。
舞蹈强调手形的优雅和足部的灵巧，
提腕勾脚，屈膝出胯，
身体成优美的"S形"，
这就是孔雀舞经典的"三道弯"。
挺直胸背，扬起下巴，
步态轻盈稳健，
这是模拟孔雀在林中漫步；
时而抖肩，时而亮翅，
头颈灵动活泼，
这是效仿孔雀在水中嬉戏。

每逢当地传统节日，
人们就会打起象脚鼓，
吹起芦笙，敲响大锣，
跳起这优雅的孔雀舞，
祈盼生活幸福美满。

傣族孔雀舞柔韧如水，挺拔如竹，
一舞千年，绵延不断。
中华五十六个民族各美其美，
传统的民族文化在传承中
不断焕发着新的生机！

补注·延伸

蒲蛮一种……四时庆吊，大小男女皆聚，吹芦笙，作孔雀舞，踏歌顿足之声震地，尽欢而罢。

——《顺宁府志》

婚娶长幼跳蹈，吹芦笙为孔雀舞。

——杨慎（明）
《南诏野史》

谁知道孔雀舞具有这么强烈的感染人心的力量啊！那翩翩柔和的舞姿、那含情脉脉的眼神，充满了和平善良的精神，感动得持刀的刽子手们松掉了屠刀，那些残忍愚昧的心灵，仿佛被圣洁的泉水洗涤过一次似的。

——《中国民间故事集成·云南卷》

Dai Peacock Dance

扫码观看视频

Among Chinese folk dances, an ethnic one is inspired by peacocks—the Dai Peacock Dance.

The Dai people living in southwest China's Yunnan Province are good singers and dancers. They regard the peacock as an auspicious "holy bird", and the peacock dance is the most famous local dance.

Thousands of years ago, Dai ancestors imitated the postures of peacocks and created this beautiful dance. During Eastern Han Dynasty (25AD-220AD), an envoy brought the dance to the capital city Luoyang. With the efforts of generations of dancers, the Dai Peacock Dance was formed and passed down to this day.

Most peacock dances are solos, but duets do exist. The dance emphasizes the grace of the hands and the dexterity of the feet. Twist your body into a beautiful "S-shape", the classic "three curves" of the peacock dance. Straighten your chest, lift your chin, and walk light and steady gait—this is to simulate a peacock walking in the forest; shake your shoulders, spread your arms, and turn your neck deftly—this is to imitate a peacock playing in the water.

At every traditional festival, the Dai people will play elephant-foot drums, blow lushengs, ring gongs and dance this graceful dance, praying for a happy life.

Pliable as water and straight as bamboos, the Dai Peacock Dance has lasted thousands of years. With the beauty of fifty-six Chinese ethnic groups, new vitality has been growing out of the inheritance of traditional culture.

蚕丝织造技艺

蚕丝织造

扫码观看视频

悠悠五千年,时光荏苒。
绫罗绸缎,锦绡绢纱,
一缕缕蚕丝编织起整个"锦绣中华"。

中国是世界桑蚕业的发源地。
相传在五千多年前的远古时期,
黄帝之妻嫘祖发明了养蚕制丝之法,
把野蚕移入室内饲养,
于是家家栽桑养蚕,春蚕吐丝,
便有了丝绸的华贵与美丽。

蚕丝织造是中国的原创性发明,
并对人类文明产生了深远影响。
生产过程包括
栽桑、养蚕、缫丝、染色和丝织等。
千百年来,织造的技艺不断发展,
在各地形成了多种流派,
各流派都有着不同的风格
和独具特色的绝活。

看!余杭清水丝绵色泽洁白,厚薄均匀;
杭罗质地轻柔滑爽,耐穿耐洗;
双林绫绢轻如蝉翼,薄如晨雾;
潞绸织造色泽光亮,绚丽多彩。
各派技艺以口传心授的方式
世代沿袭不绝,
成为华夏民族代代流传的蚕桑文明。

蚕丝织造技艺的传播
还孕育了举世闻名的"丝绸之路"。
长河落日,大漠孤烟,
一方小小的丝之经纬,
一路绵延,
传播了中华文明,
促进了东西方经济、文化交流。
纤细不过毫厘的蚕丝,
织就了独属于中华民族的锦绣华章。

补注·延伸

春日载阳，有鸣仓庚。女执懿筐，遵彼微行。爰求柔桑。春日迟迟，采桑祁祁。

——《诗经·豳风·七月》

民之通于蚕桑，使蚕不疾病者，皆置之黄金一斤，直食八石。谨听其言，而藏之官，使师旅之事无所与，此国策之大者也。

——管仲（春秋时期）
《管子·山权数》

桑出罗兮柘出绫，绫罗妆束出娉婷。娉婷红粉歌金缕，歌与桃花柳絮听。

——唐伯虎（明）
《题桑》

柔桑感阳风，阿娜婴兰妇。垂条付绿叶，委体看女手。
春蚕不应老，昼夜常怀丝。何惜微躯尽，缠绵自有时。
绩蚕初成茧，相思条女密。投身汤水中，贵得共成匹。
素丝非常质，屈折成绮罗。敢辞机杼劳，但恐花色多。

——《作蚕丝》

Chinese Sericulture and Silk

扫码观看视频

Dating back to at least 5,000 years, sericulture and silk craftsmanship is an original Chinese creation, embodying China's long history and profound culture.

Legend has it that over 5,000 years ago, Empress Leizu, wife of the Yellow Emperor, managed to domesticate silkworms and produce silk thread from the filaments. Then the knowledge of sericulture became widespread in China.

As a cultural symbol of the Chinese nation, silk craftsmanship has exerted significant influence on human civilization. Silk-making encompasses various processes such as unreeling silk, dyeing and weaving.

Silk-making has been handed down and further developed, with techniques often spreading within local groups. Each group demonstrates its unique characteristics.

In east China's Zhejiang province, a local group has developed silk that is white and pure; another group makes silk that is smooth yet tenacious; there is another style famous for its softness and lustre. Whereas silk from north China's Shanxi Province was a tribute to the imperial court. All these local styles constitute the unique silk culture of the Chinese nation.

Eventually the secret of silk spread beyond China. Goods and ideas of different civilizations travelled along the ancient Silk Road which connected China and the Far East with the Middle East and Europe.

Sericulture and silk craftsmanship have joined the UNESCO's Representative List of the Intangible Cultural Heritage of Humanity.

乌龙茶制作

扫码观看视频

叱咤饮料届的几巨头，
谁能更胜一筹？
无论是口感的丰富，
还是制作技艺的精巧，
当属茶为最。

茶叶的发酵程度不同，滋味也各有千秋。
红茶经过完全发酵，
口感醇厚，回味悠久；
绿茶往往不经发酵，
气味天然，清香爽口；
如果既想体验红茶的浓郁，
又想留住绿茶的清爽，
半发酵的乌龙茶无疑是最佳选择。

相传在清朝雍正年间，
福建省安溪县的一名茶农在采茶时，
看到了一头肥美的山獐。
一心想品尝野味的他，
不顾身背的茶篓，就去追捕那山獐。
满载而归后，他更是把制茶抛到脑后，
直到第二天才想起来。
茶叶在篓里经过剧烈的摇动，
又加上一夜的搁置，
竟散发出独特的芬芳，
冲泡起来味醇甘厚又无苦涩，
别有一番风味。

这两道颇具"乌龙"色彩的制茶工序
一直传承至今，
被称为摇青和凉青。
"摇动"与"静置"反复交替，
茶叶的边缘先得到发酵，
呈现出"绿叶红镶边"的奇特现象，
也带来了乌龙茶独特的韵味。

要品最正宗的乌龙茶，
还要到福建安溪去。
乌龙茶制作技艺目前已被列入
国家级非物质文化遗产名录，
凝结着匠人精神的安溪茶
焕发着蓬勃生机。
依靠特色茶产业，
安溪县也实现了从"贫困县"
到"全国百强县"的华丽转身，
更是获得了"中国茶都"的美誉。

补注·延伸

灵山寺茶,俗贵之。近则远购武夷。以五月至则斗茶,必以大彬之罐,必以若琛之杯,必以大壮之炉。扇必以王官溪之蒲,盛必以长竹之筐。

——《龙溪县志》

采取枝头雀舌,带露和烟捣研,结就紫云堆,轻动黄金碾。飞起绿尘埃。老龙团,真凤髓,点将来,兔毫盏里,霎时滋味,舌头回。

——苏轼(宋)
《水调歌头·咏茶》

宿雨一番蔬甲嫩,春山几焙茗旗香。

——黄夷简(宋)
《句》

漳泉各属,俗尚功夫茶,器具精巧,壶有小如胡桃者,名孟公壶,杯极小者,名若深杯。……饮必细啜久咀,否则相为嗤笑……

——施鸿保(清)
《闽杂记》

Chinese Oolong Tea Making

扫码观看视频

What is the world's most consumed beverage? Coffee? Coke? No. It's tea!

A tea leaf starts to oxidize as soon as it is plucked. Black teas are fully oxidized; green teas are swiftly processed with almost no oxidization. Between rich blacks and herby greens, a complex and intriguing semi-oxidized Chinese tea has an elegant throne of its own. It is called the oolong tea.

About 300 years ago, a tea planter in Southeast China's Anxi County suddenly started to hunt an animal while plucking tea leaves. He ran after the animal with a basket of tea leaves on his back. Focusing on the animal, he forgot to process the tea that day. Surprisingly, the next day, he found that the tea leaves gave off a fascinating aroma after being "neglected" and being "shaken" and "wounded". A new method of processing tea is thus developed.

Nowadays, the fully-developed craftsmanship of making oolong tea contains over a dozen steps, among which the essential ones include withering and bruising. As the leaves being tossed, the outer rim begins to brown, as this part is the first to be oxidized. So "the green leaf with a red rim" is a key feature of the semi-oxidized oolong tea.

Today, with the government's support on preserving and developing intangible cultural heritage, the once impoverished Anxi County in Fujian province has been lifted out of poverty, developing a modern tea industry. As China's tea capital, Anxi is making the world's best varieties of oolong tea.

景德镇制瓷技艺

景德镇制瓷

扫码观看视频

"中华向号瓷之国，瓷业高峰是此都。"
"此都"指的就是景德镇，
位于江西省东北部。
千余年来，这里形成了
独具特色的手工制瓷工艺生产体系，
创造了中国陶瓷史上
最灿烂的一段历史。

景德镇自五代时期开始生产瓷器，
到了宋代，
景德镇的瓷业已初具雏形。
明、清以后，
形成了众多的手工业工场，
景德镇由此成为陶瓷大都会，
为瓷业习俗的最终形成
奠定了坚实的基础。
景德镇手工制瓷工艺的
行业分工极其细致，
核心的工序包括拉坯、利坯、
施釉、画坯和烧窑等。
拉坯是成型的最初阶段，
是用轮制成型的方法
制成一定形状和尺寸的坯件。
利坯是将粗坯经过两次旋削，
使原本的粗坯厚度适当、表里一致。
施釉是在器坯内外涂上一层玻璃质釉，
使它更加光润。
画坯是用青花料在坯胎上绘画，
打青花箍或写上青花字。
烧窑是成瓷的最后一道关键工序，
需要用一天一夜的时间，
把坯胎烧成瓷胎。

景德镇瓷器也以
"白如玉，明如镜，薄如纸，声如磬"
的独特风格享誉海内外。
景德镇的瓷器品种齐全，
其中的青花瓷、玲珑瓷、粉彩瓷、色釉瓷
被称为景德镇四大传统名瓷。
正是景德镇得天独厚的
气候特点、瓷土资源和森林资源等
自然条件，
奠定了景德镇作为"瓷都"的历史地位。

补注·延伸

共计一坯之力,过手七十二,方克成器。其中微细节目,尚不能尽也。

——宋应星(明)
《天工开物》

青如天,明如镜,薄如纸,声如磬。

——文震亨(明)
《长物志》

中华向号瓷之国,瓷业高峰是此都。

——郭沫若
《题与艺术瓷厂》

Porcelain Making in Jingdezhen

扫码观看视频

A representative of China is its delicate porcelain. And the world's porcelain capital is Jingdezhen in east China's Jiangxi Province. The city's handmade porcelain has gained worldwide recognition. Here in Jingdezhen, the story of porcelain is still being told.

Artisans in Jingdezhen have been making porcelain since the Five Dynasties Period (907-960). The techniques matured in the Song Dynasty (960-1279). Then in the next few centuries, with many famous workshops emerging, Jingdezhen gradually developed into a porcelain capital, setting the standards for porcelain making.

The sophisticated processes of making porcelain in Jingdezhen include wheel throwing, fine trimming, glazing, painting, firing, etc. During wheel throwing, the craftsmen place the clay on a spinning base and transform it into certain shapes. Then various tools, like knives, are used to rub or polish the clay body to ensure an even thickness. The glaze made up of quartz, kaolin and other minerals, is applied to make the porcelain glow. Decorative patterns or Chinese characters are painted on the clay body as well. The perfection of the porcelain depends upon the firing, during which the clay body is fired for at least 24 hours.

Jingdezhen porcelain is dubbed "as white as jade, as bright as a mirror, as thin as paper, and also as tuneful as a bell".

The four classic types of Jingdezhen porcelain include the blue-white porcelain, the rice pattern porcelain, famille rose, as well as the color-glazed porcelain.

The natural environment of Jingdezhen, including its mild climate and abundant clay resources, has helped make Jingdezhen the world's porcelain capital.

白酒酿制

扫码观看视频

琼浆玉液,名不虚传;
九域香馨,一枝独秀。
中国白酒以酒香渗入千年文化。

酱香型白酒,
以酒体醇厚、优雅细腻著称,
《史记》中记载,
建元六年(公元前135年),
汉武帝派遣唐蒙出使南越,
唐蒙喝到南越所产的枸酱酒后,
将这种酒带回了长安。
到了明末清初,
匠人们用大曲参与糖化、发酵、
蒸馏取酒的工艺日趋成熟,
经过不断改良,
便有了如今举世闻名的酱香型白酒。

清香型白酒,
甘润爽口,余味柔和。
清代中期,一些烧酒作坊
为了提高烧酒的质量,
用锡锅对酒进行冷却。
因为第一锅和第三锅冷却的酒
带有部分杂质,
所以只保留第二次换入锡锅
冷却流出的最为纯净的酒,
就得到了绵甜清爽的清香型白酒。

浓香型白酒,
香气馥郁,回味悠长,
具有上百年历史的老窖池
是浓香型白酒酿制技艺的根基。
老窖池经过长期使用,
窖泥会形成微生物,
与酒醅共同发酵。
池中蒸馏出的酒
也就有了芬芳浓郁的味道。

如今的白酒犹如
中国发给世界的一张飘香的名片,
淋漓尽致地展现出了
中华酒文化的魅力和韵味!

补注·延伸

酒冠黔人国,盐登赤虺河。

——郑珍(清)
《茅台村》

建元六年(公元前135年),大行王恢击东越,东越杀王郢以报。恢因兵威使番阳令唐蒙风指晓南越。南越食蒙蜀枸酱,蒙问所从来,曰"道西北牂柯,牂柯江广数里,出番禺城下。"蒙归至长安,问蜀贾人,贾人曰:"独蜀出枸酱,多持窃出市夜郎。"

——司马迁(汉)
《史记·西南夷列传》

茅台酒,仁怀城西茅台村制酒,黔省称第一。其料用纯高粱者上,用杂粮者次。制法:煮料和曲即纳窖中,弥月出窖烤之,其曲用小麦,谓之白水曲,黔人称大曲酒,一曰茅台烧。仁怀地瘠民贫,茅台烧房不下二十家,所费山粮不下二万石。

——《遵义府志》

一座茅台旧有村,糟邱无数结为邻。使君休怨曲生醉,利锁名缰更醉人。于今酒好在茅台,滇黔川湘客到来。贩去千里市上卖,谁不称奇亦罕哉。

——张国华(清)
《竹枝词·茅台村》

按黔省所产之酒,以仁怀茅台村之高粱酒最佳。郑子尹诗所谓"酒冠黔人国"也。

——《贵州通志》

Chinese *Baijiu* Distilling

扫码观看视频

"Superb liquor, it lives up to its name; a unique fragrance, from this wonderful land." The aroma of Chinese *baijiu* has infiltrated the long history of Chinese culture.

Moutai-flavor liquor features a mellow and delicate taste. It is recorded in history that Han Dynasty Emperor Wu dispatched an envoy in the sixth year of his reign (135 BC) to a town in southern China. After drinking the liquor produced there, the envoy brought it back to the capital city Chang'an (today's Xi'an). In the late Ming and early Qing Dynasties, the process of using distiller yeast in saccharification, fermentation and distillation had gradually matured. After continuous improvement, the world-famous Moutai-flavor *baijiu* was produced.

Fen-flavor *baijiu* is refreshing with soft aftertaste. In the mid-Qing Dynasty, some workshops cooled the liquor in tin pots to improve its quality. Only the purest liquor cooled in the pot for the second time was kept. That light-aroma type is called Fen-flavor *baijiu*.

Luzhou-flavor *baijiu* has a strong aroma and lingering aftertaste. Old cellars exceeding a century in age provide the foundations for making Luzhou-flavor *baijiu*. The old cellars, after a long time in use, produce a special aroma thanks to the fermented microorganisms in the distilled liquor.

Today, Chinese *baijiu* is billed as a "business card" of China, showing the charms of China's drinking culture!

扬派盆景技艺

扬派盆景

扫码观看视频

盆景，顾名思义就是"盆中之景"。
融"诗、书、画、技"为一体，
聚"山、水、树、景"于一盆。
盆景创作源于自然，又高于自然。

扬派盆景发源于江苏扬州。
以天然植物为主要素材，
凭借人工置景手艺，
把江南的园林美景浓缩在方寸空间内。

扬派盆景形成于明代，兴盛于清代。
鼎盛时期，
当地"家家有花园，户户养盆景"。
其中，最出名的技艺叫作"一寸三弯"，
指造型最密处，
一寸树枝内可以有三处弯曲。

盆景中的古树名木造型不一，
有的清奇古怪，有的气韵生动。
枝条千回百转，
像是盘旋着的龙，
又像古朴的画，
被中国文人称为"无声的诗"。

盆景是时间的艺术，
需要长期经营，细心管理。
好的作品往往要花费几年、
几十年时间去创作和维护。
作为中国的传统艺术之一，
盆景凝聚着创作者的
艺术趣味与人生感悟，
展示出独特的中华古典园林韵味。

补注·延伸

至于蟠结，柯干苍老，束缚尽解，不露做手，多有态若天生。

——屠隆（明）
《考槃馀事》

至扬州，获二石，其一绿色，冈峦迤逦，有穴达于背；其一玉白可鉴。渍以盆水，置几案间。

——苏轼（宋）
《双石（并引）》

去年扬州梅数株，红红白白才须臾。中有一盆六尺余……

——张之翰（元）
《谢谭学正送盆梅》

Yangzhou *Penjing*

扫码观看视频

Penjing, as its name suggests, is "landscape in a pot". It integrates "poetry, calligraphy, painting and artistry", and builds "mountains, water, trees and landscape" in one pot. *Penjing* is created from nature and beyond nature.

Originating in east China's Jiangsu Province, Yangzhou *penjing* takes natural plants as the main material, and condenses the beauty of gardens south of the Yangtze River into small space with artificial skills.

Yangzhou *penjing* originated in the Ming Dynasty (1368-1644) and flourished in the Qing Dynasty (1644-1911).

In its heyday, "every local family had a garden, and every household kept their *penjing*". The most famous technique is called "three bends in one inch": there can be three bends within one inch of a branch. The trees in *penjing* are in different shapes. Some are quirky; some have special charm. The branches have twists and turns, either like a coiling dragon, or like an ancient painting. *Penjing* is called "silent poetry" by Chinese literati.

As an art of time, *Penjing* requires long-term care and careful management. It often takes years or decades to create and maintain a *penjing* work. As one of the traditional Chinese arts, *penjing* embodies the creator's artistic interest and life perception, and the unique charm of classical Chinese gardens.

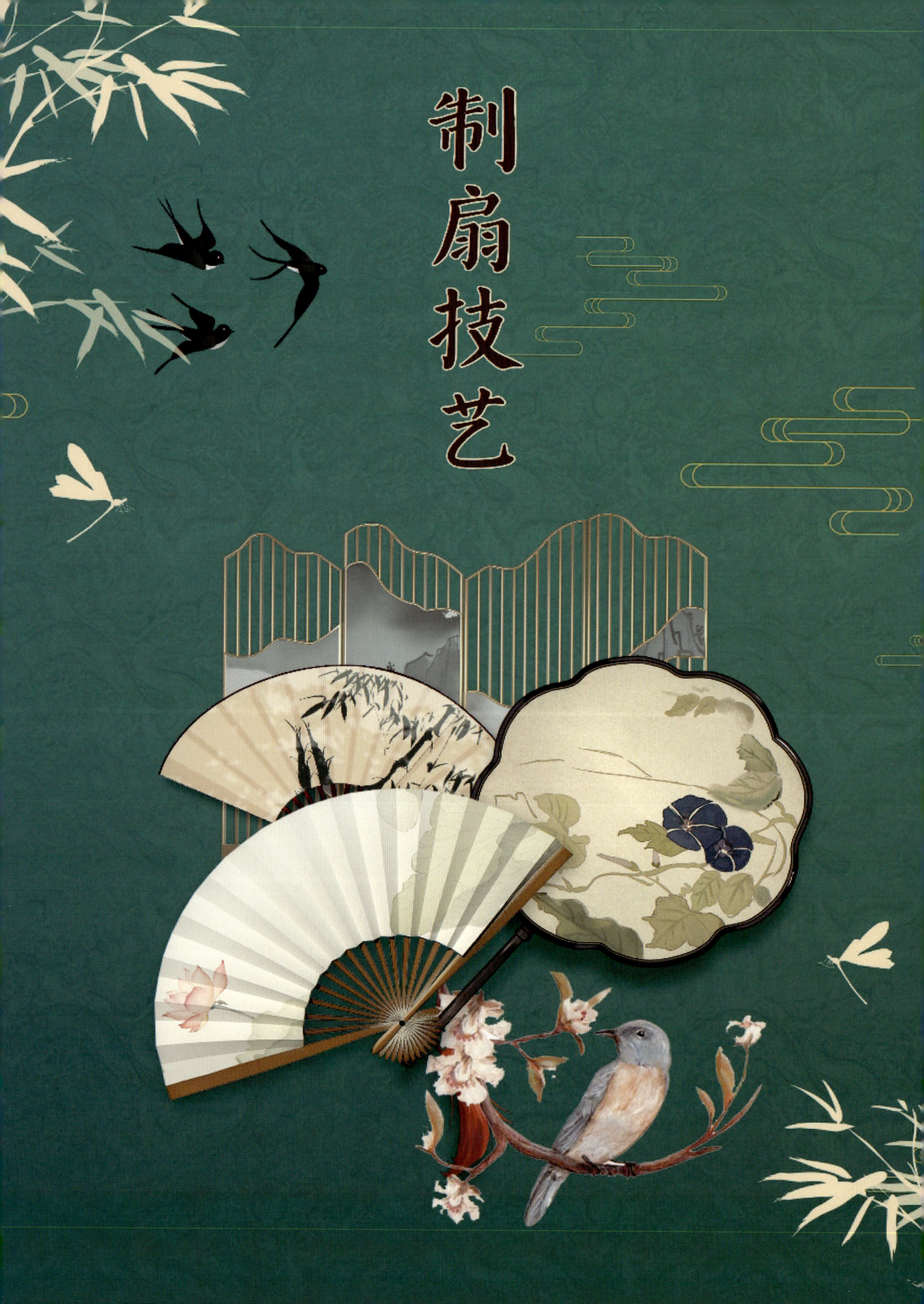

制 扇

扫码观看视频

扇子,
是夏日里摇动生风的清凉工具,
也是备受中国文人喜爱的怀袖雅物。

中国制扇技艺集雕刻、绘画、书法、
编织、装裱、髹漆等多种工艺为一体,
是一种珍贵的民族艺术形式。
千百年来,
能工巧匠凝聚本土智慧,
形成了复杂精细的制作工序。

用木头、竹子、骨头等制成扇骨,
羽毛、绢纱、竹篾、棉料、宣纸等做扇面。
设计长圆、扁圆、葵花、梅花、六角等
多样的造型,
并搭配扇坠、流苏、玉器等精巧的挂饰,
品类丰富、工艺精巧、造型优美的
扇子就出现在了人们面前。

文人墨客把佩戴扇子作为一种时尚,
不同品种的扇子也彰显着不同的气质。
折扇收放自如,富有诗书之气;
羽扇生风柔和,尽显淡然从容;
绢宫扇精巧雅致,书画刺绣别出心裁;
黑纸扇古朴典雅,坚韧耐用堪比"半把伞";
檀香木扇精美绝伦,打开扇子清香四溢;
竹篾丝扇图案鲜明,花鸟人物精细生动。

小小一把扇,
实用性与艺术性兼备,
凝聚古今工艺美术之精华,
描绘中国山水、人物与历史,
尽显中国古老深邃的文化气韵。

补注·延伸

尝画团扇,上为山川。咫尺之内,而瞻万里之遥;方寸之中,乃辩千寻之峻。

——姚最(南北朝)

《续画品》

素是自然色,圆因裁制功。飒如松起籁,飘似鹤翻空。盛夏不销雪,终年无尽风。引秋生手里,藏月入怀中。麈尾斑非疋,蒲葵陋不同。何人称相对,清瘦白须翁。

——白居易(唐)

《白羽扇》

姑苏最重书画扇,其骨以白竹、棕竹、乌木、紫白檀、湘妃、眉绿等为之,间有用牙及玳瑁者,有员头、直根、绦环、结子、板板花诸式,素白金面,购求名笔图写,佳者价绝高。

——文震亨(明)

《长物志》

Fan Making

扫码观看视频

The fan, a tool that brings coolness in summer, is an elegant accessory loved by Chinese literati.

Chinese fan-making skills integrate carving, painting, handwriting, weaving, mounting, lacquering and other crafts into one, and it is a precious national art form. Over thousands of years, skilled craftsmen have made a complex and delicate fan-making process with their wisdom.

The fan frame can be made of wood, bamboo or animal bones. And the material is feathers, silk, bamboo skin, cotton or rice paper. The fan can be designed into oval, oblate, sunflower, plum blossom, hexagonal or other shapes, and matched with knots, tassels, jade or other pendants. The mixture brings a touch of far Eastern chic to you.

Chinese literati wear fans as a fashion accessory, as different fans create different styles. The folding fan folds easily and gives an air of poetry and books. The feather fan creates gentle wind and an air of lightness and calmness. The silk palace fan is delicate and elegant, with ingenious calligraphy, painting or embroidery. The black paper fan is simple and graceful, its durability comparable to "half an umbrella". The sandalwood fan is exquisite, its fragrance overflowing when opened. The bamboo stripe silk fan has vivid pattern of fine flowers, birds and figures.

A small fan, both practical and artistic, condenses the essence of ancient and modern crafts, and depicts Chinese landscapes, figures and history. It is an epitome of the ancient and profound Chinese artistic flavor.

烟火爆竹制作

扫码观看视频

爆竹声中皆故事,
人间烟火有味道。
中国是世界上最早发明火药的国家,
而以火药制作的烟火爆竹,
同样是中国古人的智慧结晶。

旧时人们认为,
竹筒燃烧爆裂的声音能够
惮赫鬼魅、祛除不详,
这应该是爆竹的由来。
南北朝时期的《荆楚岁时记》
就记载了百姓在庭前
燃竹筒、避恶鬼的习俗。
隋唐后,人们在竹筒中装入火药,
使用更加方便快捷。
宋代,人们改用纸包裹火药燃爆,
爆竹的技术一次次得到发展。
明清两代,爆竹发展出双响震天雷、
二踢脚、飞天十响等著名品种。
烟火又名"焰火""礼花"等,
是人们在追求声音的享受之外,
对光、影、形的又一种追求。
唐代时已经出现"火药什戏烟火",
明代烟火品种更多。

时光流逝,
人类的思想和文化逐渐进步,
爆竹和烟火的制造
也逐步发展出繁多的花样,
在工艺上也演化出卷筒、切筒、糊底、
灌泥、引火药、封眼等多种技术,
呈现出的图案、花样也越来越丰富。
爆竹响,烟花繁,
辞暮尔尔,烟火年年,
在极具观赏性的同时,
将节日的喜庆气氛推向高潮,
尽显中国劳动人民辟邪除灾、
迎祥纳福的美好愿望,
承载着国人心中无法磨灭的情结
和不可言明的感动。

补注·延伸

爆竹声中一岁除,春风送暖入屠苏。

——王安石(宋)
《元日》

夜未央,庭燎之光。

——无名氏
《诗经·小雅·庭燎》

楚人重岁时,爆竹鸣磔磔。

——苏辙(宋)
《辛丑除日寄子瞻》

竹爆广庭,松标高户。

——韩鄂(唐)
《岁华纪丽·元日》

Fireworks Making

扫码观看视频

China is where gunpowder was invented. Firecrackers, made of gunpowder, is also wisdom of ancient Chinese people.

People used to believe that the sound of bamboo tubes bursting can scare off ghosts and evil. This should be the origin of firecrackers. After the Sui (581-618) and Tang Dynasties (618-907), people put gunpowder in bamboo tubes, which could be burnt more quickly. In the Song Dynasty (960-1279), people used paper to wrap gunpowder. In the Ming (1368-1644) and Qing Dynasties (1644-1911), firecrackers had famous varieties such as Thunderous Double-Crack, Double-Bang, and Flying Ten-Crack. Fireworks show people's pursuit of light, shadow and shape in addition to the enjoyment of sound.

As time passed by, fireworks have been further diversified. Various technologies have been applied such as Tube-rolling, tube-cutting, bottom pasting, clay filling, powder priming and hole-sealing. The patterns are also increasingly rich.

When fireworks are set off, people ring out the old year and ring in the new. The fireworks are highly ornamental and bring the festival atmosphere to a climax. This fully shows the good wishes of the Chinese people to ward off evil and welcome good fortune, and carries the indelible sentiment and emotion in their hearts.

风筝制作

扫码观看视频

风筝,是人类最早的飞行器。
相传,两千多年前的中国人就已经
能够借助风筝放飞人类的飞行梦想了。
凭借着奇思妙想和放飞实践,
人类一直在不断创造形态各异的风筝,
独特的制作技艺也层出不穷。

相传,
风筝最初主要用于军事目的。
到了唐代,
风筝逐渐成为一种娱乐活动。
到了宋代,
风筝制作也成了一种专门的手艺。
明清时期,
风筝制作技艺达到了鼎盛。
放风筝更是成了一种时尚,
当时的文人常常亲手扎绘风筝,
以"筝"会友,极具风雅。

风筝制作技艺集多种手工艺于一体,
除了扎作骨架、裱糊、彩绘等基本环节,
不同地区的风筝制作技艺也各具特色。
天津风筝通过打眼扣榫的骨架结构
让风筝更加自然立体;
南通板鹞风筝创造性地添加了哨口,
放飞时常伴有美妙的声音;
潍坊风筝最有名的设计是"龙头蜈蚣",
头大身长,气势恢宏;
北京风筝采用特殊的"脱胎"技艺
使风筝栩栩如生;
拉萨风筝的放飞技巧则体现在
放线与收线的变化之间,
形成风筝在空中的争斗玩耍之姿。

风筝匠人们将传统文化与各地特色
倾注于制作工艺中,
铸就了中国特有的风筝制作技艺体系。
"儿童散学归来早,忙趁东风放纸鸢。"
细细的风筝线串起中国孩子的童年,
一收一放间,
也牵动着无数穿越时空的欢声笑语。

补注·延伸

清明，小儿女作纸鸢、秋千之戏。纸鸢其制不一，于鹤、燕、蝶、蝉各类外，兼作种种人物，无不惟妙惟肖，奇巧百出。

本邑每逢寒食，东门外，沙滩上……板桥横亘，河水初泮，桃李葩吐，杨柳烟含，凌空纸鸢，高入云端。

——《潍县志稿》

纸花如雪满天飞，娇女秋千打四围。五色罗裙风摆动，好将蝴蝶斗春归。

——郑板桥（清）

《怀潍县》

雨余溪水掠堤平，闲看村童谢晚晴。竹马踉蹡冲淖去，纸鸢跋扈挟风鸣。

——陆游（宋）

《观村童戏溪上》

一百四日小寒食，冶游争上白浪河。纸鸢儿子秋千女，乱比新来春燕多。

——郭麟（清）

《竹枝词》

放鸢清明日，斗鸡寒食天。

——民间歌谣

Kite Making

扫码观看视频

Kite, the earliest aircraft in the world, is said to have been made and flown by Chinese people 2,000 years ago. Extraordinary imagination and repeated test flights enable humans to keep creating kites of many different shapes and advancing distinctive crafts.

In ancient times, kites were originally used for military purposes. It was in the Tang Dynasty (618-907) that kite-flying gradually became a leisure activity. Kite-making turned into a professional craft in the Song Dynasty (960-1279) and reached its climax from the 14th century to early 20th century. Flying kites gained popularity at that time. It was deemed graceful for literati to make kites and meet friends with a shared interest in kites.

The kite-making process includes various crafts such as structuring, paperhanging, and color-drawing. Apart from these basic crafts, the workmanship of kites is regionally characterized. Tianjin kites stand out for the three-dimensional structure resulting from the tenon and mortise framework. Nantong kites named "Banyao" are creatively installed with whistles that can make beautiful sounds when flying. Weifang kites are most famous for the large and magnificent "dragon-head centipedes". Beijing kites adopt special bionics technique to create lifelike shapes. In Lhasa, people play kite-fighting by flexibly changing the length of the kite string.

Kite artisans put Chinese traditional culture and local characteristics into their crafts, making the kite craftsmanship unique to China.

As the poem line goes, "Children return home in haste after school, eager to fly kites when there is yet wind." The flying kites have always been a part of our sweet memory in childhood.

传统香制作

扫码观看视频

天气晴朗的时候，
福建的广场上总是晒满了
五颜六色的永春香。
据统计，东南亚地区每三根香，
就有一根曾在永春县晒过太阳。
点上一炷香，在香气袅袅中
"闻香识永春"。

在中国，香文化历史悠久，
焚香则被誉为"十大高雅之首"，
古代文人雅士们"无香不足以为聚"。
写诗要焚香，赏花要焚香，
待客、休息都要焚香，
香在人们的生活中可谓
如影随形、无处不在。

永春香流传至今，最讲究的是"手艺"。
上等的香甚至需要两三代人的调试。
沾水打底、展香、抡香、切香……
十多道工序必不可少。

用天然香料和中草药配制成的香品
还原了草木的芬芳；
还形成了竹签香、盘香、塔香等
不同的形制。

时至今日，永春制香人仍虔诚地
坚持着传统的手艺。
"以香为名"也成了
当地人取名的特色。
良姜，奇楠，
这些好听的名字其实都是制香的原料。
"以香为名"浪漫又真挚，
人们爱香敬香，代代相传。

来自阿拉伯的香料
沿着"海上丝绸之路"漂洋过海，
与中国传统香文化在福建永春县相遇。
在文化的碰撞中创造出了
独特的永春香。

补注·延伸

不是闻思所及,且令鼻观先参。

——苏轼(宋)
《和黄鲁直烧香二首其一》

香者,乃天地之正气也。

——《神农本草经》

泉南佛国天下少,满城香气栴檀绕。

——释宗泐(元)
《清源洞图为洁上人作》

焚香入兰台,起草多芳言。

——李白(唐)
《赠宣城赵太守悦》

Traditional Incense Making

扫码观看视频

When it is sunny, colorful Yongchun incense is always sun-baked on squares in Fujian. According to statistics, for every three incense sticks in Southeast Asia, one of them comes from Yongchun County.

In China, the culture of incense has a long history. Incense-burning is known as the "top of ten elegant deeds". The ancient literati "would not gather without incense burning". They used incense when writing poetry, appreciating flowers, entertaining guests and resting. Incense is everywhere in ancient people's lives.

The most important thing for Yongchun incense is its "craftsmanship". It even requires two or three generations of people for improvement. More than ten procedures are essential in this process, including soaking in water as a base, extending, swirling and chopping.

The products made from natural spices and Chinese herbal medicines can restore the fragrance of plants and wood. They also have different forms (bamboo stick incense, coiled incense, tower incense, etc).

To this day, the incense makers in Yongchun are still devoted to the traditional craftsmanship. "Naming with incense ingredients" has also become a custom of local people. Liangjiang (galangal), Qinan (Aquilaria Crassna), these names are actually the raw materials for incense. "Naming with incense" is romantic and sincere, showing people's love and respect for incense from generation to generation.

Spices from Arabia crossed the sea along the Maritime Silk Road, encountered with Chinese incense culture in Yongchun County. The unique Yongchun incense was then created in the exchange of cultures.

传统民居营造技艺

传统民居营造

扫码观看视频

红砖白石,燕尾屋脊,
镶嵌着精美的木石雕刻装饰。
独特风格的红砖古厝,
是闽南地域建筑色彩中的主旋律。
透露着浓厚民俗气息的同时,
也将大量建筑技艺、知识汇于一身。

闽南传统民居营造技艺是中原文化
和闽南本土文化相融合的产物,
始于唐五代,
是闽南地区古建筑技艺的主流,
传播于闽南文化圈的泉州、漳州、
厦门和台港澳、东南亚地区,
细分为大木作、小木作、砖石作、
瓦作、彩画、堆剪作等工种。
俗称"皇宫起"的官式大厝
即这种营造技艺最为典型的类型。

相传"皇宫起"源于晚唐五代时期,
当时闽王的嫔妃黄厥系惠安人,
因得闽王宠爱而被特许按宫殿规制
和外形在家乡大兴土木,
"皇宫起"由此成为当地民居
争相仿效的建筑样式,
并逐渐流传四方。

明艳动人的红砖外墙,
檐角高翘的精妙屋脊线——燕尾脊,
别出心裁的承重结构,
无一不显示出
当地工匠灵巧独到的手艺,
将闽南传统民居奇妙绚丽的色彩
展现在世人眼中,
并伴随闽南人的足迹,远播海内外,
让中华民族瑰宝一路绵延,熠熠生辉。

补注·延伸

保护好传统街区，保护好古建筑，保护好文物，就是保存了城市的历史和文脉。对待古建筑、老宅子、老街区要有珍爱之心、尊崇之心。

——习近平总书记在福建考察时的重要讲话

秩秩斯干，幽幽南山。如竹苞矣，如松茂矣。兄及弟矣，式相好矣，无相犹矣。似续妣祖，筑室百堵，西南其户。爰居爰处，爰笑爰语。约之阁阁，椓之橐橐。风雨攸除，鸟鼠攸去，君子攸芋。如跂斯翼，如矢斯棘，如鸟斯革，如翚斯飞，君子攸跻。殖殖其庭，有觉其楹。

——《诗经·小雅·斯干》

Traditional Dwellings in Southern Fujian

扫码观看视频

Red bricks, white stones and swallow-tailed ridges are decorated with exquisite wood and stone carving. The unique red-brick houses are the main architecture in southern Fujian. While revealing the strong traditional culture, it also brings together architectural knowledge and craftsmanship.

The traditional dwellings in southern Fujian integrated the cultures of the Central Plains and Minnan areas. Created in the 10th century, it has been the mainstream of ancient architectural techniques there. Then it was also spread to Quanzhou, Zhangzhou, Xiamen, Taiwan, Hong Kong, Macao and Southeast Asia. It is subdivided into timber framework, brick and stone work, tile-making, color-painting and other skills. The aulic residence "Huanggongqi" is the most typical of this construction technique.

"Huanggongqi" is commonly known as "Imperial Palace-Style Building". At that time, one of the beloved concubines (Huang Jue) of the King (the King of Min, Fujian) was allowed to build large palace-style buildings in her hometown, Hui'an. The style was then imitated by local dwellings, and gradually spread to other areas.

Bright red bricks of the exterior wall, the exquisite ridge with curving eaves-"Swallowtail Ridge", ingenious load-bearing structure (Chuandou-style timber structure), all of them show the unique craftsmanship of local builders and bring the gorgeous traditional houses in southern Fujian to the world. Along with the footprints of people from southern Fujian, it has spread far and wide, making Chinese national treasures continue and shine all the way.

牛羊肉烹制

扫码观看视频

牛羊肉的烹制,
可算是被中国人给玩明白了。
除了北京的东来顺涮羊肉、
"南宛北季"烤牛羊肉、
月盛斋酱烧牛羊肉,
还有山西冠云平遥牛肉、内蒙古烤全羊
和宁夏手抓羊。
可谓五花八门。

东来顺的涮羊肉有
选料精、调料香、糖蒜脆、火锅旺等特点,
只要将羊肉片放入汤中,稍涮片刻就熟了。
东来顺涮羊肉肥而不油、瘦而不柴,
一涮即熟、久涮不老,
吃起来不膻不腻、味道鲜美。
怪不得北京人常说"涮肉何处嫩,
要数东来顺"。

阿拉善烤全羊,
是内蒙古自治区阿拉善盟特有的美味佳肴,
是游牧民族智慧的产物。

阿拉善烤全羊采用土种绵羯羊,
经过当地植物梭梭的烤制,
烤出的肉以色、香、味、形俱佳而闻名。

北京月盛斋创建于清乾隆三十年,
以酱牛肉和烧羊肉而闻名。
酱牛肉使用的香料既能调味,
又有药用价值,
做出的肉品不仅味道鲜美,
而且具有滋补养生的功效。
月盛斋烧羊肉讲究火候,
除了选料、配方和独一无二的
兑老汤技术外,
又有验料、选材、调汤、煮制等
约二十道工序。
日午烧来焦且烂,喜无膻味腻喉咙。

各式各样的牛羊肉烹制技艺
有的源于宫廷,有的来自民间。
它们不仅凝聚了中国劳动人民的智慧,
也成了中华美食文化中的瑰宝。

补注·延伸

烹羊宰牛且为乐，会须一饮三百杯。

——李白（唐）

《将进酒》

苏文熟，吃羊肉；苏文生，吃菜羹。

——陆游（宋）

《老学庵笔记》

（羊肉）暖中补虚，开胃健力，滋肾气，养肝明目，健脾健胃、补肺助气。

——李时珍（明）

《本草纲目》

煨羊肥嫩数京中，酱用清汤色煮红，日午烧来焦且烂，喜无膻味腻喉咙。

——杨静亭（清）

《都门杂咏》

Beef and Mutton Cooking

扫码观看视频

Chinese people are masters of cooking beef and mutton. In Beijing, there are Donglaishun mutton hotpot, grilled beef and mutton in "Nan Wan Bei Ji", sauced beef and braised mutton from Yueshengzhai. Meanwhile, there are also corned beef from Shanxi, Inner Mongolia roast whole lamb and Ningxia-style mutton (eaten with hands). How diverse the cooking techniques are!

Donglaishun is characterized by high-quality mutton, fine flavors, crispy sugar garlic, and a very hot pot. Just put the mutton slices into the pot, and it will be instantly-boiled. The mutton is fatty but not greasy, or lean but not tough. It is cooked within seconds but the good taste is long-lasting. No wonder people in Beijing often say:"To find the tender mutton, you must go to Donglaishun."

Roasted Whole Lamb is a unique delicacy in Alxa, Inner Mongolia Autonomous Region, also a product of nomadic wisdom. The roasting process is fueled by the local plant Haloxylon and only native sheep are used. The roasted lamb is famous for its excellent look, aroma and taste.

Yueshengzhai was founded in Beijing in 1775, famous for sauced beef and braised mutton. The spices used have good flavor and medicinal value. The beef is both tasty and nutritious. Heating control is essential for braised mutton. Other than the unique selection of ingredients, recipe and soup-mixing technology, about 20 steps are required such as material checking, mutton choosing, braising…

Some of these cooking techniques originate from the royal court, others from the common people. They embody Chinese people's wisdom, and become a treasure in Chinese food culture.

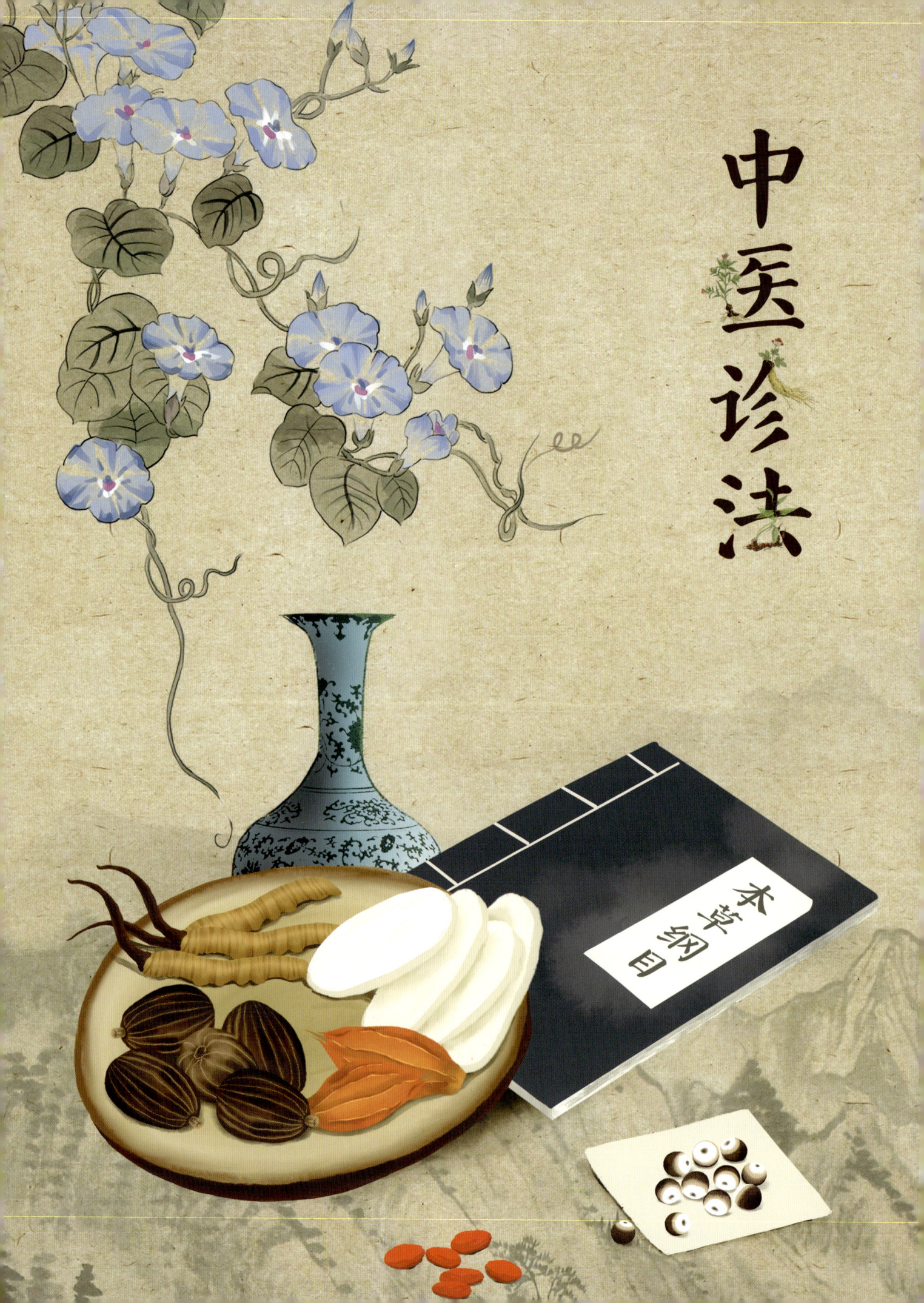

中医诊法

扫码观看视频

公元 2 世纪,
医圣张仲景在瘟疫中
写就了著名的中医书籍《伤寒杂病论》。
20 世纪 70 年代,
中国科学家屠呦呦从中医中获得灵感,
发现了能消灭疟疾的青蒿素,
拯救了无数人的生命。
诞生于中华大地的"中医学"
在漫漫历史长河中,
护佑着中华民族延续千年。

"辨证论治"是中医的灵魂,
古人对生命现象的长期观察
和大量临床实践,
创造了一系列诊疗理论,
其中,望、闻、问、切
是中医诊断的四大法宝。

中草药则是中医处方的主角,
明代药学家李时珍的《本草纲目》
记录了 1892 种药材,附图 1109 种,
被誉为"古代中国的百科全书"。

中医讲究治标治本,更要防患于未然。
东汉末年,
华佗模仿虎、鹿、熊、猿、鸟
五种动物的动作发明了"五禽戏",
既能舒展身心,又能预防疾病。
中医讲究内部调养,
但外科手术也绝非西方医学的专利。
早在公元 2 世纪,
中国古代医者就创制了
用于外科手术的麻沸散,
可以减轻病人在治疗中的痛苦。

在没有 X 光、心电图的古代,
中医诊法在文明的延续中
发挥着重要作用。
在现代医学和科学的发展中,
博大精深的中医学
依然绽放着独特的魅力。

补注·延伸

坚持中西医并重和优势互补，大力发展中医药事业。健全中医药服务体系，发挥中医药在疾病预防、治疗、康复中的独特优势。加强中西医结合，促进少数民族医药发展。加强古典医籍精华的梳理和挖掘，建设中医药科技支撑平台，改革完善中药审评审批机制，促进中药新药研发保护和产业发展。强化中药质量监管，促进中药质量提升。强化中医药特色人才培养，加强中医药文化传承与创新发展，推动中医药走向世界。

——《中华人民共和国国民经济和社会发展第十四个五年规划和2035年远景目标纲要》

中国医药，既云渊源于道家，而道家又以精微博大著称，其学术自当别自高明，奈何近世以来，一遇西洋医药输入，举国之人，几视其为陈腐朽败不经之学，将欲尽弃而勿论之耶？

——南怀瑾

西医是身体观，中医是生命观。

——梁漱溟

治病须分内外科，世间妙艺苦无多。神威罕及惟关将，圣手能医说华佗。华佗仙术比长桑，神识如窥垣一方。惆怅人亡书亦绝，后人无复见青囊！

——《三国演义》

TCM Diagnostic Methods

扫码观看视频

In the second century, Zhang Zhongjing, wrote this classic of traditional Chinese medicine (TCM), *Shang han za bing Lun* (*Treatise on Febrile and Other Diseases*), when epidemic infectious illnesses were prevalent.Decades ago, inspired by TCM, Tu Youyou managed to extract artemisinin which inhibits the malaria parasite, saving millions of lives. For thousands of years, traditional Chinese medicine has been an essential part of the health care system in China.

"Syndrome differentiation", known as the soul of TCM, is the process of comprehensive analysis of clinical information obtained by the four main TCM diagnostic methods—inspection, listening & smelling, inquiry, and pulse-taking & palpation.

One of the treatment methods is to use herbal medicines. Chinese pharmacologist Li Shizhen (1518-1593) compiled and wrote *Ben cao gang mu* (*Compendium of Materia Medica*), which lists 1,892 medicinal substances. This medical encyclopedia was the first of its kind in the world.

Traditional Chinese medicine also focuses on health maintenance. Over 1,800 years ago, Hua Tuo studied the movements of animals, developing the Exercise of the Five Animals, namely, tiger, deer, bear, ape and bird.

Apart from being a physician and herbal expert, Hua Tuo, who lived in the second century, was also a surgeon. He is best known for his surgical operations and the use of *mafeisan*, an anesthetic formulation made from herbs.

Traditional Chinese medicine contains extensive knowledge that the Chinese people have accumulated through practical experimentation and theoretical research in treating diseases and promoting health. It continues to play a vital role in the modern world.

汉字书法

汉字书法

扫码观看视频

挽袖运笔，泼墨挥毫，
汉字书法，就在这一笔一画中，
展现出中华文字的独特魅力。

商代中后期的甲骨文与金文，
是目前我国发现的最早的汉字资料。
从夏、商、周到西汉的漫长历史传承中，
形成了篆、隶、草、行、楷五种书体。

中国人常说"见字如晤""字如其人"，
今天的我们
仍可以通过书法与古人对话。
这是郑板桥的行书，
字里行间是不拘一格的灵魂。
这是颜真卿的楷书，
一笔一画写的是刚直忠义。

这是张旭、怀素的草书，
龙飞凤舞、气势非凡，
彰显了那个时代的文人旷达不羁的性情。

晋代书法家王羲之的《兰亭集序》
被称为"天下第一行书"，
全文没有一个字写法相同，
仅一个"之"字就有十余种写法，
绝美兰亭，叹为观止。

蓦然回首，
篇篇笔墨背后，
屹立的是千年传承的文化宝库，
一撇一捺，
汉字书法写就大写的中国"人"。

补注·延伸

书法是中华文化瑰宝，包含着很多精气神的东西，一定要传承和发扬好。

——习近平

书法不过一技耳，然立品是第一关头。品高者，一点一画，自有清刚雅正之气；品下者，虽激昂顿挫，俨然可观，而纵横刚暴，未免流露楮外。

——朱和羹（清）

书尚清而厚，清厚要必本于心行，不然，书虽幸免薄浊，亦但为他人写照而已。

——刘熙载（清）
《艺概》

中国书法的地位，很占重要，它是训练抽象的气韵与轮廓的基本艺术，吾们还可以说它供给中国人民以基本的审美观念，而中国人的学得线条美与轮廓美的基本意识，也是从书法而来。故谈论中国艺术而不懂书法及其艺术的灵感是不可能的。

——林语堂
《吾国与吾民》

Chinese Calligraphy

扫码观看视频

Chinese calligraphy, was inscribed in 2009 on the list of the Intangible Cultural Heritage of Humanity of the UN Educational, Scientific and Cultural Organization.

The earliest forms of written Chinese include the 3,000-year-old oracle-bone script and the bronze script.

Then the next 1,000 years saw the development of five different styles of script, known as "seal" "official" "cursive" "running" and "regular".

Calligraphy works say quite much about the calligrapher's life, personality and morality.

The running script reflects the unconventionality of a so-called "eccentric" scholar, Zheng Banqiao.

The regular script, in which each stroke is firm and clear, mirrors the integrity of a loyal governor, Yan Zhenqing.

The cursive script, written at a very fast speed, shows the wild and unrestrained nature of the literati of the Tang Dynasty (618-907).

The most famous running script was created by Wang Xizhi. In his work which records a poetic event held at the Orchid Pavilion, the character "zhi" appears in variant artistic forms. It must have been an inspirational event at the Orchid Pavilion.

Chinese calligraphy also reflects the philosophical thinking of the Chinese people, who believe that the structure of the character "ren" (meaning "human") should be stable and upright.

剪 纸

扫码观看视频

一张纸能玩儿出什么花样？
古老的中国剪纸给出了答案。
精巧雅致的扬州技法，
粗犷凝练的安塞风格，
从南到北，
在辽阔的中原大地上
诞生了各种各样的剪纸流派，
用剪刀将纸裁成千变万化的图案。

早在春秋战国时期，
"镂空雕刻"的技法
就被运用于工艺品的制作当中。
真正意义上的剪纸艺术
产生于造纸术之后。
相传在汉朝，
一个书生随手写下一个"福"字，
妻子把它撕了出来，
这就成了剪纸的前身。

北朝团花剪纸是最早的
且有据可查的剪纸形态，
在几何形团花之外，
剪出对马、对猴等图案，
刀法简练，具有古朴浓郁的民间风格。
随着剪纸技艺的不断进步，
剪纸在颜色上有了单色和多色的区分，
纹样也发展出了人物、鸟兽、山水等
多个种类，
承载着人们的生活意趣和美好愿景。
看，这莲花抱鲤鱼的图样，
不就是千年流传的祝福——
"连年有余"吗？

一张红纸，
一把剪刀，
剪出的是代代相传的
中国普通百姓的勤劳智慧。
快拿起纸与剪，
创造属于你的趣味剪纸吧！

补注·延伸

正月七日为人日,以七种菜为羹,剪采为人,或镂金箔为人,以贴屏风,亦戴之头鬓,又造华胜以相遗。

——宗懔(南北朝)
《荆楚岁时记》

立春日,俗间悉剪彩为燕子,置之檐楹,亦戴。贴宜春之字……七日名为人日,家家剪彩或镂金箔为人,以贴屏风,亦戴之头鬓。今世多刻花胜,象瑞图、金胜之形。

——杜台卿(隋)
《玉烛宝典》

雪圃乍开红菜甲,彩幡新翦绿杨丝。殷勤为作宜春曲,题向花笺帖绣楣。

——韦庄(唐)
《立春》

立春日,自郎官、御史、寺监长贰以上,皆赐春幡胜,以罗为之。宰执、亲王、近臣,皆赐金银幡胜。入贺讫,戴归私第。

——孟元老(宋)
《东京梦华录·卷六·立春》

曾见北国之窗花,其味天真而浑厚。今见南方之刻纸,玲珑剔透得未有。一剪之趣夺神功,美在民间永不朽。

——郭沫若
《剪画选胜》

Chinese Paper Cutting

扫码观看视频

What can be done with a piece of paper? Chinese paper cutting is the answer, with delicate and elegant style from Yangzhou and concise style from Ansai. Ancient China has given birth to a wide variety of paper-cut styles. People cut the paper into diverse shapes with their scissors.

Early in the 1st century BC, "Hollow-out carving" was used in making handicrafts. The paper cutting art came into being after paper was invented around 2,000 years ago. A young man wrote down the character "fu", and his wife tore it out. This became the predecessor of paper-cutting.

Tuanhua in the 1st century is the earliest documented form of paper cutting. Besides round blossoms, symmetrical horses and monkeys were also cut out. With the improvement of skills, paper-cuts developed into multi-colored ones, and diversified patterns, such as figures, beasts and landscapes, carrying people's interests and vision of life. Look at this pattern of the lotus surrounding the koi! Isn't it people's wishes for a better life?

A piece of red paper and a pair of scissors stand for the diligence and wisdom of Chinese people. Pick up your paper and scissors, and create your own paper cutting!

料 器

扫码观看视频

北京料器是一种中国传统手工艺品，
色彩斑斓，造型各异。
从小巧精致的鼻烟壶
到端庄灵动的花鸟摆件，
一块块莹润的琉璃在匠人的巧手中
变成了精美的料器。

据记载，
早在明代，京城元宵节灯会上
就出现了料器花灯。
清朝康熙年间，北京琉璃厂设置了
专为皇室制造料器的御厂。
因此在当时料器又被称为"宫料"，
也叫"御琉璃"。
清朝衰落后，
料器制造由宫廷转入民间，
渐渐形成了浓郁的北京特色。

北京料器历经二百多年的发展，
以工艺精细著称。
工艺师将料棍在灯上加温烧软，
用镊子、剪刀等抻、拉、拽、粘，
造型全在工艺师脑子里，
凭空塑造出想要的形象，
凭经验一次成型。
生肖动物、佛像、花鸟、骆驼，
这些大大小小的料器艺术品，
每一件都是独一无二的。

精美的料器凝聚着
中国匠人的巧思与心血。
北京料器不仅是精美绝伦的手工艺品，
还是兼具艺术性与文化性的民族瑰宝。

补注·延伸

向夕而张灯,灯则烧球,料丝则夹画、堆墨等。

——刘侗(明)、于奕正(明)
《帝京景物略》

料丝出于滇南,以金齿卫(今保山市)者为胜。用玛瑙、紫石英诸药捣为屑,煮腐如粉,必市天花菜点之方凝,然后取之为丝,极晶莹可爱。

——赵翼(清)
《陔余丛考》

两边大梁上挂着联三聚五玻璃彩穗灯,每席前竖着倒垂荷叶一柄,柄上有彩烛插着。这荷叶乃是洋錾珐琅活信,可以扭转向外,将灯影逼住,照着看戏,分外真切。窗格门户,一齐摘下,全挂彩穗各种宫灯。廊檐内外及两边游廊罩棚,将羊角、玻璃、戳纱、料丝,或绣、或画、或绢、或纸诸灯挂满。

——《红楼梦》

Beijing Glazeware

扫码观看视频

As a traditional Chinese handicraft, Beijing glazeware is rich in color and shape. In the skillful hands of the craftsmen, pieces of lustrous glaze have been turned into exquisite glazeware, including small, delicate snuff bottles and flower and bird ornaments.

Records show glaze lanterns appeared at the Lantern Festival in Beijing as early as the Ming Dynasty (1368-1644). In the following Qing Dynasty (1644-1911), Emperor Kangxi ordered the establishment of Liulichang to produce glazeware for the royal family. So the glazeware was also called "palace" or "royal" glazeware. After the fall of the Qing Dynasty (1644-1911), the production of glazeware was mainly for the market rather than for the court, and it gradually formed a strong Beijing style.

After more than 200 years of development, Beijing glazeware is famous for its fine craftsmanship. The craftsman heats the glaze rod on the lamp to soften it, then works on it with tweezers or scissors to create the desired shape in just one go. Zodiac animals, Buddha statues, flowers and birds, camels—each of these large or small pieces of art has its own style.

The exquisite glazeware crystallizes the creative mind and painstaking efforts of Chinese craftsmen. It is not only a fabulous handicraft, but also a national treasure with both artistry and culture.

景泰蓝

扫码观看视频

景泰蓝，又叫铜胎掐丝珐琅，
是一项中国传统工艺。
你看，原本光秃秃的器皿，
有了景泰蓝的加持，
一下子就变得精致华丽、
栩栩如生起来。

相传，景泰蓝工艺起源于元代，
到了明朝景泰年间趋于成熟，
成品以蓝色为主，
因此得名"景泰蓝"。
在古代，
景泰蓝因为用料昂贵、工艺烦琐，
很长一段时间都是皇家专属。

仔细观察，这些精美的纹饰
都是匠人们用一根根
发丝般细软的扁铜丝
掐成各种花纹焊上去的。
在铜质的胎型上
填入多彩的色釉进行烧制，
接着进行磨光、镀金，
最后的景泰蓝成品色泽鲜亮、端庄大气。

景泰蓝纹饰丰富，生动多姿。
有"龙凤呈祥""暗八仙"
这样栩栩如生的图画；
也有"福、寿、喜"这样简洁大气的文字；
还有寄托信仰的佛教图画等。

景泰蓝集中华历史、文化、艺术于一身，
代表了我国手工艺品制作的高超技艺，
也体现了手工艺人的匠心和精神。

补注·延伸

大食窑出大食国,以铜作身,用药烧成五色花者,与佛朗嵌相似。尝见香炉、花瓶、盒儿、盏子之类,但可妇人闺阁之中用,非士大夫文房清玩。世又谓之鬼国窑,今云南人在京多作酒盏,俗呼曰鬼国嵌。内府作者,细润可爱。

——王佐(明)
《新增格古要论》

予得一瓶,以铜为胚胎,傅之以革,外为觚棱,彩绘外国人之奇形诡状,却似琉璃,极其工巧,不知为何物。

——顾文荐(宋)
《负暄杂录》

Jingtailan (Cloisonné)

扫码观看视频

Jingtailan, also known as filigree enamel with copper mold, is a traditional Chinese craft. The vases, kettles and other objects may seem a little bit dull at the beginning, but become exquisite artworks with the *Jingtailan* decorations.

Originating in the Yuan Dynasty (1206-1368), it thrived in the Ming dynasty (1368-1644) during the reign of the Jingtai Emperor (1449-1457), when a new blue pigment was discovered and gave *Jingtailan* its current name based on the Chinese word "lan" for blue. It used to be exclusive to the imperial families.

The making of *Jingtailan* requires rather elaborate processes. Use red copper to make a mold, and weld copper wires on the copper mold according to the drawn pattern. Next, inlay glaze into the empty space of the pattern. After repeated enamel-firing, polishing and gilding, an exquisite *Jingtailan* product is made.

Traditional *Jingtailan* patterns include paintings of the auspicious Chinese dragon and phoenix, Chinese characters for sending good wishes as well as Buddhist images.

Nowadays, *Jingtailan* artworks often serve as China's gifts to foreign leaders and international institutions, conveying Chinese people's best wishes to the world.

布艺老虎

扫码观看视频

老虎是威风凛凛的百兽之王，
可你见过它们萌态十足的样子吗？
请看这只布老虎——
头大、眼大、嘴大、尾巴大，
既不失老虎本身的威武，
又透出几分孩童的天真。

布艺老虎是中国传统的针线手艺，
起源于祖先对虎的崇拜。
《山海经》中就记载过这样一个故事，
传说一对神将兄弟曾率虎群与恶鬼搏斗，
保住了成熟的仙桃与神树，
惠及一方百姓。
老虎的名声也随之大震，
成为坚强、勇敢的象征。

布艺老虎的制作包括剪、缝、装瓤、绣、扎、画等多种工序，
制作的材料及工艺也各不相同。
较为常见的是用棉布、丝绸缝制成形，
内填谷糠、棉花等物，
再描绘上五官和花纹。

心灵手巧的老一辈制作布老虎
作为玩具、摆件，
陪伴小孩左右。
布艺老虎是中国孩子的"泰迪熊"，
装点着他们的童年，
见证着他们的成长。

布艺老虎体现着中国人
特有的心灵手巧和聪明才智。
一针一线，
都是对下一代满满的爱意与祝福。

补注·延伸

虎者,阳物,百兽之长也。能执搏挫锐,噬食鬼魅。

——应劭(汉)

《风俗通义·祀典》

西方金也,其帝少昊,其佐蓐收,执矩而治秋。其神为太白,其兽白虎。

——刘安(汉)

《淮南子》

Cloth Tiger

扫码观看视频

The tiger is the majestic king of beasts, but have you seen how cute they are? Look at this cloth tiger—big head, big eyes, big mouth and big tail. It does not lose the might of the tiger, but reveals a bit of childish innocence.

Cloth tiger is a traditional Chinese needle and thread craftsmanship, originating from the ancestors' worship of the tiger. *Shan Hai Jing* (*The Classics of Mountains and Seas*) The legend has it that two god brothers led a group of tigers to fight against evil spirits, and preserved the sacred trees and peaches for the people in that area. The tiger's reputation has thus been made, and it has become a symbol of strength and bravery.

The production of cloth tigers includes cutting, sewing, furnishing, embroidery, tying and painting. Various materials and craftsmanship are used. They are often made with cloth or silk, stuffed with cotton or grain bran, then the facial features and stripes are painted.

The older generation makes cloth tigers as toys and ornaments for children. They are Chinese children's "Teddy Bears", furnishing their childhood and witnessing their growth.

They also embody the ingenuity and originality of the Chinese people. Every stitch is full of love and blessings for the next generation.

面 花

扫码观看视频

既是雕塑作品，也是一道美食。
面花，在寒冷的冬天依然盛开。
面花塑作艺术主要流行于
中国北方地区，
与当地劳动人民的饮食、习俗息息相关。

在中国古代，
人们把面团做成各色动物、花卉，
代替真正的动物供奉祖先和神明。
后来，面花制品越来越丰富，
兼具了食用与观赏的多种功能，
逐渐在传统佳节、婚丧嫁娶等
场合中扮演更重要的角色。

面花塑品大到三五斤，小到三五寸，
造型风格贴近百姓生活。
捏制石榴、莲花、桃子等
喜庆形状的面花
是许多地区春节期间的保留节目；
还有的面花会被做成京剧脸谱的样式，
小小面团摇身一变，
成为生、旦、净、丑等戏曲角色。

制作面花的工具同样来源于生活。
锥子、梳子等器物
都可以用来压出点、线，
成就精巧的纹饰。
各地风土人情不同，
面花也带有鲜明的地域特色。
比如工艺复杂、制作精巧的黄陵面花；
简单大方、追求写意的新绛面花；
具有浓郁乡土气息的郎庄面花等。
中国北方的民间艺术家们
用一双巧手诉说着
他们所热爱的家乡与生活。

补注·延伸

宴诸司以面及药蓊之类,染作颜色,用像豚肩、羊、脍炙之属,皆逼真也。

——王谠(宋)

《唐语林》

用面造枣䭅飞燕,柳条串之,插于门楣,谓之"子推燕"。

以油面糖蜜造为笑靥儿,谓之果实。

——孟元老(宋)

《东京梦华录》

上元,以面作盏,蒸作灯,边捏月份,按其干湿卜旱涝。

——《威海卫志》

Dough Modelling

扫码观看视频

It is both a sculpture and a delicacy. The dough flower can still bloom in the cold winter. The art of dough modelling is popular in northern China, closely related to the diet and customs of the local people. In ancient China, people modelled the dough into shapes of animals and flowers to worship ancestors and gods in place of real animals. Later, dough sculpture has been varied, with both edible and ornamental functions. Gradually, they played a more important role in traditional festivals and weddings.

The sculptures can be as heavy as two kilos or as small as three inches. The designs are close to people's life. Making dough sculptures of lotus flowers, peaches and other festive decorations is a custom during the Spring Festival in many regions. Some of the dough sculptures are roles of Peking Opera: Sheng (male lead); Dan (female lead); Jing (male with painted face); and Chou (clown).

The tools for dough modelling are also common in most homes. Awls, combs and other utensils can be used to press out points and lines, helping create exquisite designs. As the local customs are different, dough modelling has regional characteristics. For example, Huangling style has complex craftsmanship and exquisite production. Xinjiang style is simple and elegant like freehand sketches. Langzhuang style maintains a strong local flavor. Folk artists in northern China depict the home and life they love with a pair of skillful hands.

面 人

扫码观看视频

提到"面",可不只有
喷香松软的面包、蛋糕,
这个栩栩如生的小人儿,
竟然也是用"面"做成的。
这就是已有一千三百多年历史的
中国传统手工技艺"面人",也叫"面塑"。
它把面粉从小小厨房搬到了艺术殿堂。

面人的制作一般先采用
捏、搓、揉、掀等手法塑造大体形制,
再用竹刀刻画细节,加以点缀。
巧手之下,面人活灵活现,栩栩如生。

面人的基本形制分
"签举式"和"案置式"两种,
"签举式"面人深受小朋友喜爱,
下方插有一根小木棍,
可以拿在手里,好吃又好玩;

"案置式"多是精致考究的陈设艺术品,
制作时在原料中混入专用添加剂,
作防裂防霉处理,
使饱含心血的面塑艺术品
能够风采长存。

"核桃面人"以径寸之室,
装入人物、鸟兽,
罔不因势象形,各具情态。
小小的核桃里,
展现了精巧的传统戏剧场景,
两半一合,就是唱念做打的戏曲世界。

热爱生活的中国人取面粉为材,
用勤劳的双手塑造出
一个个美好的艺术形象。
欢欢喜喜举个面人回家,
是许多中国人难忘的童年记忆。

补注·延伸

以油面糖蜜造如笑靥儿。

——孟元老（宋）
《东京梦华录》

大拇指头大小的风筝，黄豆大小的花脸面具，绿豆大小的空钟，半个米粒大小的小白鸭子，小米大小的糖球……我真不知他是怎么捏的，会捏得这么小，这么可爱！

——冰心

Dough Figurine

扫码观看视频

Not only the savory, fluffy bread and cakes, but this lifelike little figurine is made from dough. This is the traditional handicraft "mianren", also known as "dough figurine", which has a history of more than 1,300 years in China. It takes the dough from a small kitchen to the hall of art.

The artisan first shapes its general form by pinching, rubbing, kneading, lifting and other methods, then uses a bamboo knife to embellish it with details.

The basic form of the dough figurines are two types: "stick-holding" and "desk-setting". The "stick-holding" ones are very popular among children. A small stick is inserted at the bottom so that the toy-like figurines can be held in hand; "Desk-setting" ones are mostly exquisite works of art for display. Special additives are mixed into the raw materials to prevent cracking and mildew and to preserve the charm of the artworks for a long time.

"Walnut dough figurines" depict legendary stories, human figures, birds and beasts, all tiny but vividly shaped within the size of a walnut. Inside little walnuts, traditional theatrical scenes are modelled delicately.

Chinese people, who love their life, take flour as the ingredient and create great artistic images with their diligent hands. Joyfully holding a dough figurine home is the unforgettable memory of childhood for many Chinese people.

糖　画

扫码观看视频

你见过可以吃的"画"吗？
来了，这是中国传统民间手工艺
——糖画。
以勺为笔，以糖为墨，
流淌间便可勾画世间万物。

相传，唐代大诗人陈子昂很爱吃黄糖，
不过他的吃法与众不同。
他将糖熔化在清洁光滑的桌面上，
铸成各种小动物图案，
等糖液凝固后便拿在手上，
一边赏玩一边品尝。
后来，陈子昂到京城长安游学求官，
也把这种吃法带到了京城，
从此糖画这门手艺代代相传。

到了清代，糖画更加流行，
制作技艺日趋精妙，
形态多为花鸟鱼虫、福禄寿喜、
十二生肖等，
都是大众喜闻乐见的吉祥图案。

糖画是一门集合了
美食、文化和手工制作的艺术，
既可观赏，又可食用，
作画师傅通常无须底稿，一气呵成。
如今的糖画出现了更多的创新形式，
卡通糖画、立体糖画，
为传统糖画带来了新的生机。
中国之文化，糖画之精神，
在一代代匠人的糖勺之间慢慢流传。

补注·延伸

以白糖煎化，模印成人物狮象之形者为饗糖。《后汉书》注所谓猊餹是也。

——李时珍（明）
《本草纲目》

炼沙糖和牛乳为石蜜（即乳糖也），唯蜀川作之。

——唐慎微（宋）
《证类本草》

液蜜为人始自汉，印成袍笏气轩昂。狻猊敛足为同列，李耳卑躬属并行。枵腹定知无肺腑，虚心自应没肝肠。儿童尽与相亲近，丞相无嗔可徜徉。熔就糖霜丞相呼，宾筵排列势非孤。苏秦录我言甘也，林甫为人口蜜腹。霉雨还潮几屈膝，香风送暖得全肤。纸糊阁老寻常事，糖丞来年亦纸糊。

——褚人获（清）
《坚瓠补集》

其人挑木柜两个，一头上扎一架，小糖熬化成汁，用模子两块合在一处，用力吹之，能成禽兽，幼童纷纷争买之。

——《北京民间生活彩图》

Sugar Painting

扫码观看视频

Have you ever eaten a "painting"? Here it is, the traditional Chinese folk art—sugar painting. Spoon as pen, liquid sugar as ink, everything in the world can be sketched through the stroke.

It is said that Chen Zi'ang, a great poet in the seventh century (Tang Dynasty), liked to eat brown sugar. But he ate it in a unique way. He melted the sugar on a clean and smooth table, and cast it into various shapes of small animals. After cooling down, it could be held in hand, eaten and enjoyed.

Later, Chen went to the capital city (Chang'an), bringing this art to the capital. Since then, sugar painting became a lasting craft.

In the 17th century (Qing Dynasty), sugar painting became more popular, and the production techniques were more sophisticated. The sugar painting could be flowers and birds, fortune symbols and the 12 zodiac signs and other designs.

The art of sugar painting combines food culture and handicraft, both ornamental and edible. The painting is done in one go without any draft. Today's sugar painting is more creative in forms, including cartoon sugar painting, 3D sugar painting, bringing new life to traditional ones.

泉州花灯

扫码观看视频

一年一度元宵明,其乐融融闹花灯。
泉州花灯,又名"灯彩",
在当地方言中,
"灯"与"丁"读音相近,
点亮花灯,
也是点亮百姓对人丁兴旺、
家庭和睦的殷殷期盼。

根据制作方式的不同,
泉州花灯可分为彩扎灯、
刻纸灯和针刺无骨灯三类。
或描画,或刀刻,或针刺,
精妙的制作技艺让泉州花灯名扬八方,
为世人称奇。

山水风景、亭台楼阁,
飞禽走兽、历史传说,
通过传统匠人的巧工细琢,
都能活灵活现地再现在小小花灯上。

泉州花灯的历史源远流长,

中国民间自古便有传统,
正月十五开灯祈福、祭拜神明。
后来唐代战乱,北方汉人纷纷南下,
闹花灯的习俗也随之迁入闽南地区,
点花灯成了百姓思念亲人、
故土的重要寄托,
便催生了泉州的花灯工艺。

时至今日,每逢元宵佳节,
花灯仍是必不可少的环节之一。
人们在屋前檐下挂灯,
成群结队上街赏灯,
小朋友提着花灯走街串巷,
猜测灯上的谜语,
好一片喜庆祥和的景象!

正月里来中国旅行,
记得去灯会看一看。
看那厚重的岁月,
流转于一盏盏轻盈的花灯,
年复一年,熠熠生辉。

补注·延伸

泉州花灯品种色色俱全,莲花灯、百花灯、琉璃灯、彩扎灯……

——梁克家(宋)

《三山志》

天下上元,灯烛之盛,无逾闽中。

——谢肇淛(明)

《五杂俎》

穷工极巧,造灯十架,凡两年成。

——张岱(明)

《陶庵梦忆》

上元灯——市人制灯出沽,或以五色纸,或以料丝,或扎通草,作花草人物虫鱼,燃以宝炬,惟妙惟肖,俗名古灯。恒于府治西畔双门前作灯市。

——陈德商(清)

《温陵岁时记》

Quanzhou Festive Lanterns

扫码观看视频

Once a year, the Lantern Festival is cheerfully celebrated with people lighting lanterns. Quanzhou festive lanterns, also known as "Deng Cai". In the local dialect, the pronunciation of "deng" (light) is similar to "ding" (population). Lighting up the lanterns means lighting up people's earnest wishes for a growing and harmonious family.

In terms of the production methods, Quanzhou lanterns can be divided into three categories. Colored bamboo lanterns, paper-cutting lanterns and perforated boneless lanterns. The exquisite craftsmanship has made Quanzhou lanterns famous and amazing to the world.

Landscape, pavilions, birds and beasts, historical legends, all of them can be vividly reproduced on a small lantern by the artisans.

Quanzhou lanterns date back to ancient times. On the fifteenth day of the first lunar month, lanterns were lighted to pray for blessings. During the war in the mid-8th century, the northern people moved to the south, bringing with them the custom of lighting up lanterns. The lanterns became an important symbol of family and hometown which promoted the lantern art in Quanzhou.

Nowadays, lanterns are still an essential part for every Lantern Festival. Families hang lanterns under the eaves of their houses. People go to the streets to enjoy the lanterns. Children walk through the streets, trying to solve the riddles written on the lanterns. What a peaceful and joyful festival!

Don't forget to visit the lantern fair, if you travel to China in the first lunar month. Look! The colorful lanterns are shining so brightly year after year.

木版年画

扫码观看视频

春节快乐,该贴年画了。
这是木版年画,
已经有一千多年的历史了,
它来自中国神话中保卫家园的门神,
在民间深受欢迎。

到了宋代,
随着城市生活的繁荣,
年画也越来越流行,
在百姓眼中,不贴年画就不算过年,
不同地域也诞生了风格各异的年画。
河北武强年画,粗犷朴实;
苏州桃花坞年画,工整细腻;
四川绵竹年画,色彩明艳。

年画既是一种传统,
又是一种生活方式。
它的主题可不仅限于新年祝福,
还有历史故事、传奇人物、
文学名著等,包罗万象。

年画记录了中国古代的社会生活,
对于历史研究也有极大的价值。
木版年画吸收了
中国古代雕版印刷术的精髓,
匠人们个个身怀绝技。

拿桃花坞木板年画来说,
制作流程就分为画稿、刻板、
印刷等五道工序,
其中刻板一项就需要十八般武艺,
使用多种刀法,讲究角度和力度,
同样一块版印刷出来的效果风格
也会因人而异,
这正是年画手艺的魅力所在。

木版年画历史悠久,
但也不是一成不变的老古董,
如今许多手艺人对木板年画的
内容进行了创新。
时代变迁,
不变的是勤劳勇敢的中国人民
对美好生活的向往与努力。

补注·延伸

上令画工摹搨镌板,印赐两府辅臣各一本。是岁除夜,遣入内供奉官梁楷就东西府给赐钟馗之象。

——沈括(宋)
《梦溪笔谈》

近岁节,市井皆印卖门神、钟馗、桃板、桃符,及财门钝驴、回头鹿马、天行帖子。卖干茄瓠、马牙菜、胶牙饧之类,以备除夜之用。

——孟元老(宋)
《东京梦华录》

上敕待诏高克明等图画三朝盛德之事,人物才及寸余,宫殿、山川、銮舆、仪卫咸备焉。命学士李淑等编次序赞之,凡一百事,为十卷,名《三朝训鉴图》。图成,复令传摹镂版印染,颁赐大臣及近上宗室。

——郭若虚(宋)
《图画见闻志》

Woodblock–Printed *Nianhua*

扫码观看视频

To celebrate Spring Festival, the Chinese people put up *nianhua* on doors. Woodblock-printed *nianhua*, or New Year Wood-block Painting, has a history of more than a thousand years. It drew inspiration from god of Doors who protect people's houses in Chinese mythology and is welcomed by people.

In the Song Dynasty (960-1279), *nianhua* gained popularity as cities flourished. It became an indispensable part of the New Year and developed various styles in different regions. Wuqiang *nianhua* in Hebei Province is wild and unpretentious. Taohuawu *nianhua* in Suzhou is known for exquisite techniques, and Mianzhu *nianhua* in Sichuan Province is renowned for its bright and vivid colors.

Nianhua is not only a traditional craft but also a lifestyle. Apart from New Year wishes, the themes of *nianhua* also include historical stories, legendary figures, classic literature and so on.

Nianhua records social life of ancient China, which makes it highly valuable for historical research. The woodblock-printed *nianhua* takes advantage of ancient Chinese woodblock printing, and the artisans have unique skills.

Take Taohuawu woodblock-printed *nianhua* as an example. The production procedures include outline drawing, image engraving, printing, etc. Just to engrave the board, it takes complex preparation, various carving methods, and careful choice of angle and strength. Even the same wood board can be printed in diversified styles by different people, which shows the charm of the *nianhua* technique.

Though having a long history, woodblock-printed *nianhua* is not stuck in a rut. Nowadays, many artisans have introduced new things to the content of woodblock-printed *nianhua*. Though time changes, what remains unchanged is Chinese people's endeavors for a better life.

建筑彩绘

扫码观看视频

色彩，能产生什么妙用？
在建筑美学与色彩美学的精彩碰撞下，
建筑彩绘的每一抹色彩，
既能延长建筑寿命，
又独具东方气韵。

中国传统建筑技艺，
在几千年的进化和传承中，
一方面它的结构很有特色，
另一方面就是各地建筑彩绘
风格各异、特色鲜明。

手法和用料，
或浓墨重彩，或淡雅飘逸。
各种颜料和土、石、木、
布、纸、陶等材料，
都是他们的创作手段。

建筑彩绘集实用性、
装饰性和观赏性于一体，
诉说着中华五千年的
历史沉淀和文化积累。

在清代，
以龙凤为图案主题的和玺彩画，
将宫殿、坛庙等建筑群主殿
装饰得金碧辉煌；
以旋花为标志性图案的旋子彩画，
为官衙、庙宇、牌楼和园林雕梁画栋；
图案自由丰富的苏式彩画，
使得皇家官吏住宅熠熠生辉。
建筑彩绘在门框、窗槛、
檐角、梁木之上，
打造了色彩纷呈的世界。

今天，建筑彩绘
作为中华古典艺术的瑰宝之一，
充分展现了建筑与绘画艺术的
完美结合，
向世人传递着强烈的艺术感染力和
独具东方魅力的文化内涵。

补注·延伸

木衣绨锦，土被朱紫。

——张衡（汉）
《西京赋》

屋不呈材，墙不露形。裛以藻绣，络以纶连。

——班固（汉）
《西都赋》

楹，天子丹，诸侯黝，大夫苍，士黈。

——《礼记》

Architectural Decorative Painting

扫码观看视频

Classical Chinese buildings are known for their richness of painted decoration, adding an oriental touch to the architecture. imparting a perfect blend of the aesthetics of architecture and the aesthetics of color.

For thousands of years, the craftsmanship of traditional Chinese architecture has been passed down and developed, highlighting the unique structures as well as the vivid decorative painting. Buildings in different regions display varied painting characteristics. Some are ornate with bold and bright colors, while others are painted in soft pastels. Apart from various pigments, different materials such as paper and pottery are also used.

Architectural decorative painting is both functional and ornamental, illustrating China's 5,000 years of history and culture. In the Qing Dynasty (1644-1911), Hexi painting, featuring the Chinese dragon and pheonix, was applied to the principal halls of the imperial palaces and temples; Xuanzi painting, characterized by spiral flowers, decorated government buildings and temples; whereas Suzhou style painting with diverse patterns, was used in officials' houses and gardens. The ornate doors, windows, cornices and beams present such a picturesque effect.

The colored painting decorated on traditional Chinese buildings incorporates all the best-known technical skills such as carving, coloring and embossing, representing a perfect combination of Chinese art and architecture.

吾族佳饰 维尔月

维吾尔族服饰

扫码观看视频

你去过新疆吗?
热情好客的维吾尔族人民
一定会穿着靓丽的服饰,
载歌载舞地迎接你,
相信这华丽大方的维吾尔族服饰
一定会让你移不开眼。

维吾尔族服饰花样繁多,
做工精湛,用色大胆,
极具地域特色,
通常使用鲜艳的丝绸
或毛料裁制成装,
其中最有名的是新疆艾德莱丝绸。

维吾尔族服饰
至今已有两三千年的历史。
每逢喜庆佳节,
随处可见身穿不同花色
民族服饰的维吾尔族群众。
其中,男性服饰突出衣领刺绣,
款式多为过膝长衣,
对襟、无领,宽松舒适,粗犷奔放;
女性服饰则多为宽袖、连衣裙外套、
对襟背心,
色彩对比强烈,相互衬托,
使红得更亮,绿得更翠。
搭配小方巾和小花帽,别有一番风味。

许多到新疆旅游的朋友,
都会忍不住买上几件维吾尔族传统服饰。
民族的也是世界的,
快来穿上这漂亮的维吾尔族服饰,
跳一支新疆舞吧!

补注·延伸

男子戴青缎小帽，缠以白布，故名缠头。衣绫绢山茧，长领齐袖衣，靴用香牛皮。妇人披发，戴红缎锐顶帽，缀以珊瑚、玛瑙。衣长袄，外披红敞衣。

——傅恒（清）、董诰（清）
《皇清职贡图》

衣裳是文化的表征，衣裳是思想的形象。

——郭沫若

可汗妻恪尊则"衣织成裙，披锦大袍，辫发于后，首戴金化（花）冠"。

——《魏书·吐谷浑传》

Uyghur Dresses

扫码观看视频

When you visit Xinjiang, the hospitable Uyghur people in beautiful dresses will greet you with singing and dancing. I am sure you will be greatly impressed by their colorful dresses.

Uyghur dresses, with distinctive features, are rich in variety, exquisite in workmanship and bright in color. They are usually made of bright-colored silk or wool, the most famous of which is Xinjiang Adlai silk.

Uyghur dresses have a history of two or three thousand years. The Uyghur people will wear colorful dresses at festive occasions. Men will wear gowns with collar embroidery. Ladies will wear wide-sleeved one-piece dresses and vests, whose red and green colors stand in strong contrast. They wear small kerchiefs and floret caps to match their dresses.

With their distinctive style, Uyghur dresses and accessories are high on the must-buy list of visitors to Xinjiang. When you are in Xinjiang, try on these beautiful Uyghur dresses and join a Xinjiang dance!

藏族唐卡

藏族唐卡

扫码观看视频

藏族唐卡,又称唐嘎,
是一种画在布面上
用彩缎装裱的卷轴画。
唐卡的题材以藏族文化历史
与佛教经典为主。
有展现人们生活习俗的生活画,
也有反映藏医藏药的科学画,
是藏族人民的"百科全书"。

最早的唐卡可以追溯到公元7世纪。
据《大昭寺志》记载,
吐蕃赞普松赞干布在经历一次神示之后,
用自己的鲜血绘制了《白拉姆》像,
由他的妻子文成公主亲手装帧,
这就是藏族的第一幅唐卡,
现在这幅唐卡已不复传世。

绘制一幅精美的唐卡,
通常需要花费几个月甚至几年的时间。

在采光最好的房间里,
画师们盘腿坐在绷好的画布前,
用笔尖蘸舌尖,而后画画。
勾线、着色、上金,
每下一笔都需凝神静息。
色彩是唐卡的灵魂,
唐卡的颜料来自珊瑚、朱砂、
绿松石等珍贵矿物。
这些天然的材料色彩艳丽,色质稳定,
历经数千年岁月的洗礼,
也不会褪色。

对于游牧在高山谷地之间的
藏族人民而言,
唐卡的意义与帐篷同等重要。
帐篷是温暖的家,
唐卡则是随身携带的"庙宇",
寄托着人们对美好生活的向往和期待。

补注·延伸

唐卡艺术是西藏优秀传统文化的奇葩,是中华民族民间艺术中不可多得的非物质文化遗产。推动唐卡产业发展,对于建立健全现代文化市场体系,传承发展民族优秀传统文化,促进文化事业和文化产业繁荣发展,建设重要的中华民族特色文化保护地意义重大。

——中共西藏自治区委员会办公厅 西藏自治区人民政府办公厅
《关于推动唐卡产业加快发展的意见》

Tibetan Thangka

扫码观看视频

Tibetan thangka, also known as tanka, is a scrolled painting on cotton or silk, framed with colored satin. The themes of thangka are mainly Tibetan culture, history and Buddhist classics. Some also depict people's customs or Tibetan medicine. It is the "encyclopedia" of the Tibetan people.

The earliest thangka dates back to the 7th century. According to historical records (*Jokhang Temple Chronicle*), the previous ruler (Songtsen Gampo) painted a portrait (Bai Ram) with his own blood. It was hand-framed by his wife (Princess Wencheng). Now this thangka cannot be found.

To paint a beautiful thangka, it usually takes months or even years. Sitting cross-legged in front of the canvas, the painters wet the brush on the tip of the tongue.

Each stroke requires concentration. Color is the soul of thangka. The pigments of thangka come from coral, cinnabar, turquoise and other precious minerals. These natural materials have bright and stable colors, which will not fade even after thousands of years.

For the Tibetan people, who live nomadically in the mountains and valleys, thangka is as important as the tent. A tent is a warm home, and a thangka is a portable "temple", carrying people's aspirations and expectations for a better life.

中国花鸟画

扫码观看视频

展开中国花鸟画的画卷，
喜鹊啁啾，寒梅傲雪。
鸟语花香跃然纸上，
情感志趣又暗藏其中。

花鸟画是中国传统三大画科之一，
花卉、鸟兽、鱼虫都是常见的题材。
魏晋南北朝时期，
花鸟画独立成科，
随后便蓬勃发展，大家迭出。
中晚唐的边鸾善画花鸟，精妙至极，
被称为"花鸟画之祖"。

花鸟画的画法，
有"工笔""写意""兼工带写"三种。
工笔画笔迹精妙细致，色彩鲜明；
写意画画风简练概括，意境飘然；
兼工带写，则兼有二者所长。

黄筌的《写生珍禽图》，
细笔勾勒了二十四种动物，
鸟的羽翅、龟的背甲、虫的触须……
工整写实、一丝不苟。
徐熙的《雪竹图》，
竹节挺拔，境界幽深。
黄筌之画，细腻华丽，
透着富贵之气；
徐熙笔下，落墨施彩，
却也率性豪迈；
后人称之为"黄徐异体"。

画家笔下的花鸟鱼虫，
寄托的是人与自然生物的审美关系。
梅的傲雪、兰的清雅、
竹的挺拔、菊的凌霜，
无一不是中国文人
对自然与生活的热爱。

补注·延伸

诗画本一律,天工与清新。边鸾雀写生,赵昌花传神。

——苏轼(宋)
《书鄢陵王主簿所画折枝二首其一》

故画竹必先得成竹于胸中,执笔熟视,乃见其所欲画者,急起从之,振笔直遂,以追其所见,如兔起鹘落,少纵则逝矣。

——苏轼(宋)
《文与可画筼筜谷偃竹记》

所以绘事之妙,多寓兴于此,与诗人相表里焉。故花之于牡丹芍药,禽之于鸾凤孔翠,必使之富贵;而松竹梅菊,鸥鹭雁鹜,必见之幽闲。

——《宣和画谱》

盖自智而慧者笔下有天真之悟,而惟清与静者胸中无一点之尘也。

——岳珂(宋)
《米元章四大字帖赞》

Chinese Flower-And-Bird Painting

扫码观看视频

Unfold the scroll of a Chinese flower-and-bird painting, on which magpies are chirping and plums blooming in the snow. When the singing birds and fragrant flowers appear on the painting, you may get the fun and emotions of a Chinese painting.

The flower-and-bird painting is one of the three traditional Chinese painting families. Flowers, birds, animals, fish and insects are common themes. From the 3rd century to the 6th century, the flower-and-bird painting became an independent family. Then it flourished, and many masters emerged one after another. Bian Luan in the middle and late Tang Dynasty (618-907) was good at painting flowers and birds. His works are extremely exquisite, which make him known as "the father of the flower-and-bird painting".

There are three methods of the flower-and-bird painting. Fine brushwork is meticulous with bright colours, while freehand brushwork is concise with elegant artistic conception. And the third method is the combination of fine brushwork and freehand brushwork. Huang Quan's painting *Rare Birds* vividly depicts 24 kinds of animals in fine strokes, including birds, turtles and insects. In Xu Xi's painting *Bamboos in the Snow*, the tall and straight bamboos show the aesthetic concept of the painter. The contrast of these two painting works reflect the different styles of the flower-and-bird painting.

The flowers, birds, fish and insects in the painter's works reflect the aesthetic relationship between human and other creatures. The plums in the snow, the elegance of orchids, the straightness of bamboos and the tenacity of chrysanthemums are all reflections of Chinese literati's love for nature and life.

中国山水画

扫码观看视频

中国画起源于汉代,
是我国传统的绘画形式,
通常使用毛笔蘸水彩和墨,
绘于绢绸或纸上。
山水画,是国画的重要画科之一,
仁者乐山,智者乐水,
文人雅士用自然景色寄托情思,
把情感融入大自然的美景,
通过艺术的手法表达出来。

中国山水画流派众多,
按画法风格分为青绿山水、
金碧山水、水墨山水等。
宋代画家王希孟的《千里江山图》
就是青绿山水的代表,
创作这幅画时,他只有18岁,
山水之间尽显少年意气。
画作在一幅整绢上绘制而成,
全长11.2米,
构图周密、用笔精细,
气势波澜壮阔。

如果说《千里江山图》
寄托的是初出茅庐的少年壮志,
那么《富春山居图》
沉淀的则是渡尽沧桑的人生感悟。
画家黄公望历经人生起伏,
晚年将人生与自然的
朝暮变幻运之于笔,
历时数年作成《富春山居图》,
漫长的江水,
流过浅滩、激流、高峰,
最终繁华落尽,
留白处是人生的底色。

中国山水画
如同水墨谱写的一首首壮丽的交响曲。
高山仰止,景行行止,
一笔一画,绘尽中华秀美山河。

补注·延伸

山水心匠自得处高也。

——米芾（宋）
《画史》

山水初无金碧、水墨之分，要在心匠布置如何耳。

——赵希鹄（宋）
《洞天清禄》

山有三远：自山下而仰山颠，谓之高远；自山前而窥山后，谓之深远；自近山而望远山，谓之平远。高远之色清明，深远之色重晦，平远之色有明有晦；高远之势突兀，深远之意重叠，平远之意冲融而缥缥缈缈。

——郭熙（宋）
《林泉高致》

Chinese Landscape Painting

扫码观看视频

Traditional Chinese painting originated in the Han Dynasty (206 BC-220 AD). It is usually painted on silk or paper with a brush dipped in watercolor and ink.

Landscape painting is an important pattern of Chinese painting. leaving their feelings in the scenery of mountains and rivers, the literati integrate their emotions into the natural beauty through artistic means.

There are different schools of Chinese landscape painting. It can be divided into blue-green style (blue-green style in turquoise), golden-green landscape (golden-green landscape in turquoise and gold), black-white landscape (black-white landscape in ink) and so on. The painting of Wang Ximeng *A Thousand Miles of Rivers and Mountains* is a classic blue-green style landscape in the Song Dynasty (960-1279). He was only 18 when he created this painting. His youthful spirit was fully shown on it. The painting was drawn on a whole piece of silk, with a total length of 11.2 meters.

While the previous painting is about the ambitions of the young, this one, *Dwelling in the Fuchun Mountains*, is full of insights in the painter's late years. Huang Gongwang had been through ups and downs and collected the changes of life and nature within his stroke. It took him three to four years to finish this painting. The long river flows through shallows, riptides, peaks, till the blank space in the end, representing the background of life.

Chinese landscape painting is like a magnificent symphony composed of ink and wash.

中国人物画

扫码观看视频

以形写神,神形兼备,
是中国人物画的特点。
人物画是中国画的三大画科之一,
流传千古的名画数不胜数。

东晋顾恺之作《洛神赋图》,
平静的水面上,
风姿绝代的洛神衣带飘逸、动态从容,
凌波而来,
顾盼间是对爱人的不舍与深情。

唐宋时期
是我国人物画发展的鼎盛时期,
南唐画家顾闳中作《韩熙载夜宴图》,
以长卷的方式描摹了
南唐官员韩熙载夜宴嘉宾的场景。
琵琶铮铮,画中女子舞姿婀娜,
宾客推杯换盏,酣畅淋漓,

笔触准确精微,线条流畅细腻,
色彩绚丽清雅,人物栩栩如生。

宋代画家张择端作《清明上河图》,
画中有八百多个人物,
江流城中,人游画中,
神态各异的街市行人,
凝固了北宋汴京繁华精彩的市井风貌。

与西方人物画注重写实不同,
中国人物画更重写意,
讲究以神为主,神形兼备,
把对人物性格特点的表现
寓于环境、气氛、
身段和动态的渲染之中。

卷卷中国人物画,
无声地讲述着千年文明的前世今生。

补注·延伸

图绘者,莫不明劝戒、著升沉,千载寂寥,披图可鉴。

——谢赫(南北朝)

《古画品录》

画西施之面,美而不可悦,规孟贲之目,大而不可畏,君形者亡焉。

——刘安(汉)

《淮南子·说山训》

恺之每画人成,或数年不点目精。人问其故,答曰:"四体妍蚩,本无关于妙处,传神写照,正在阿堵中。"

——《晋书·顾恺之传》

Chinese Figure Painting

扫码观看视频

To capture a person's spirit while depicting him or her is the key feature of Chinese figure painting, which is one of the three major categories of Chinese painting. Countless famous paintings have been passed down through the ages.

In the *Nymph of the Luo River* by Gu Kaizhi, the graceful river nymph descends on the gentle water waves, ribbons from her robes blowing in the wind. Her eyes are filled with attachment and affection for her lover.

The Tang (618-907) and Song Dynasties (960-1279) are the heyday of Chinese figure painting.

The *Night Revels of Han Xizai* by Gu Hongzhong depicts the scenes of a night party hosted by the Southern Tang official Han Xizai in a long scroll. With the beautiful music of *pipa* and the graceful dance of the lady, the guests entertain themselves fully, feasting and drinking. The painting is done with precise and subtle brushstrokes, smooth and delicate lines, and bright and elegant colors. The figures are lifelike.

In the *Along the River During the Qingming Festival* by Zhang Zeduan, more than 800 figures are depicted. The running Bianhe River provides a picturesque background for the pedestrians who, with different expressions and postures, solidify the flourishing urban life in the capital city of Bianliang.

While Western figure painting focuses on creating true-life depictions of the subject, Chinese figure painting emphasizes expressing the inner essence of the theme. The expression of a character's personality and disposition is embodied in the rendering of the environment, atmosphere, posture, and movement.

Scrolls of Chinese figure paintings silently tell the past and present of thousands of years of civilization.

中国篆刻

扫码观看视频

成竹在胸，一气呵成，
方寸之间，尽显中华文字之美，
这就是中国篆刻。
无论是古朴浑厚的玉玺，
还是端庄婉转的小印，
篆刻用一笔一画
勾勒出了历史的轮廓。

篆刻俗称治印，
以刀代笔，
在印章上刻画中国汉字。
秦汉时代，
玺印是权力和身份的象征。
相传，秦代丞相李斯
曾奉秦始皇之命，
用和氏璧镌刻"传国玉玺"
作为中国历代正统皇帝的凭证。

后来，篆刻的发展逐渐大众化，
被更广泛地用作署名和收藏。

时至今日，篆刻依旧流行。
篆刻不仅能够锻炼
专注力、观察力，
还能提高人的审美情趣。
一刀一印，精雕细琢。
2008年北京奥运会会徽
就是一枚古香古色的印章。

篆刻是工匠精神
和中华古典美学的结合，
一桌、一石、一刻刀，
在润物细无声中，
传承古人智慧，传播中华文化。

中国篆刻

解码中华文化基因

补注·延伸

印之佳者有三品：神、妙、能。然轻重有法中之法，屈伸得神外之神，笔未到而意到，形未存而神存，印之神品也。婉转得情趣，稀密无拘束，增减合六文，挪让有依顾，不加雕琢，印之妙品也。长短大小，中规中矩方圆之制，繁简去存，无懒散局限之失，清雅平正，印之能品也。有此三者，可追秦汉矣。

——甘旸（明）

《印章集说》

刀拙而锋锐，貌古而神虚。篆法体势方者，方易于劲（遒劲），但方并非即是劲，故要得其方劲。圆易于转（婉转），但圆并非即是转，故又要得其圆转。有方劲而无圆转，近于犷悍。有圆转而失方劲，近于媚俗。

——吴昌硕（清末民初）

《论封泥》

古人篆刻思离群，舒卷浑同岭上云。看到六朝唐宋妙，何曾墨守汉家文。

——丁敬（清）

《论印绝句》

Chinese Seal Engraving

扫码观看视频

As a cornerstone of Chinese fine arts, Chinese seal engraving manifests the beauty of Chinese characters to the utmost. From the ancient imperial seals made of jade, to the more common seals used by all, history unfolds itself through these intricate curves and lines.

The art of engraving requires mastery of calligraphy and a high degree of virtuosity. The imperial jade seals were used by the Chinese emperors as a sign of power and authority.

Over 2,000 years ago, China's first imperial seal was created for China's first emperor Qin Shi Huang. This Heirloom Seal of the Realm was carved out of Heshibi, a sacred piece of jade. Later, the seals become more widely used in lieu of signatures and as artistic collections.

Today, Chinese seal engraving still enjoys great popularity. It helps improve one's concentration and observation skills, also enabling the development of aesthetic taste. Consisting of the Chinese character "Jing" which also portrays a human figure running forward and embracing triumph, the emblem of the 2008 Beijing Olympic Games was also inspired by this art.

Chinese seal engraving is a combination of craftsman spirit and classical Chinese aesthetics, endowed with the wisdom of ancient Chinese people and the value of Chinese culture.

雕版印刷

扫码观看视频

印刷术的发明距今已有两千年的历史。
被称为世界印刷史上的
"活化石"的雕版印刷，
在今天仍然保留着它的传统魅力。

在中国古代雕版印刷发明后，
印刷术取代了手抄，
使书籍的出版变得更加高效，
推动了人类文化的发展和进步。

雕版印刷起源于唐代，
凝聚着造纸术、制墨术、
雕刻术、摹拓术等人类智慧。
唐咸通九年的《金刚经》
是现存最早的雕版印刷品。
雕刻精美、刀法纯熟、图文浑厚凝重，
可以看出当时刊刻技术
已达到极高水平。
到了宋代，刻书风行一时，
印刷品纸墨上乘，刻印精良，
有"一页宋版书，一两黄金"的说法。

雕版印刷步骤简单，但工艺精巧。
第一步，刻板。
选平滑的木板，反贴上抄写工整的书稿，
由雕刻工匠拳刀勾线，铲刀留白，
妙手回转之间，
文字便从木板之上"脱颖而出"。
第二步，拓印。
将刻好的字版均匀地涂上油墨，
覆盖上纸张，轻抚纸张背面，
那字迹便"跃然纸上"。
第三步，装帧。
将一页页印好的书稿汇聚成册，
整理校对，装订成书。

古代工匠精巧的手艺，
印刻出古老的中华文明，
多少传奇的故事
凝固成永恒的瞬间传播开来。

补注·延伸

自唐末五季以来始为印书，极于近世，而闽、浙、庸蜀之锓梓遍天下。加以传说日繁，粹类益广，大纲小目彪列胪分，后生晚学开卷了然，苟有小慧纤能，则能袭而取之。

——魏了翁（宋）
《鹤山先生大全集》

近岁市人转相摹刻诸子百家之书，日传万纸，学者之于书，多且易致，如此其文词学术，当倍蓰于昔人。

——苏轼（宋）
《李氏山房藏书记》

二十年间，禁省、观寺、邮候墙壁之上无不书，王公、妾妇、牛童、马走之口无不道。至于缮写模勒，街卖于市井，或持之以交酒茗者，处处皆是。

——元稹（唐）
《白氏长庆集序》

Woodblock Printing

扫码观看视频

Printing was invented two thousand years ago. Woodblock printing, known as the "living fossil" in the printing history, still retains its traditional charm today. After its invention in ancient China, woodblock printing replaced hand-copying, making book-publishing more efficient, and promoted the development and progress of culture.

Woodblock printing originated in the Tang Dynasty (618-907). It integrated papermaking, ink making, engraving, and copying. The earliest dated woodblock print (*The Diamond Sutra*, 868, the 9th year of Xiantong, Tang Dynasty) revealed detailed carving, heavy and dignified graphics, demonstrating the high level of printing technology. In the Song Dynasty (960-1279), woodblock printed books were quite popular. Books were well engraved with quality ink on fine paper.

The steps of woodblock printing are simple, but the craftsmanship is exquisite. First, engrave the woodblock. Choose a smooth wooden board and paste the neatly copied manuscript on the reverse side. Outline every character and leave blank space. Then the text "stands out" from the wooden board. Second, print out the text. Coat the engraved board with ink evenly, put the paper atop the board, and run the hand over the back of the paper (dip ink and paint). The handwriting will "jump onto the paper". The third step is bookbinding. The pages of the printed manuscript are gathered, collated, then bound into a book.

The ancient Chinese civilization is engraved through this craftsmanship. So many legends are printed into eternal moments and spread widely.

京　绣

扫码观看视频

穿花纳锦、描龙刺凤，
透过眼前这华美的京绣，
我们仿佛看见了历史的针脚。
京绣是燕京八绝之一，
历史上用于供奉宫廷亲贵，
以用料讲究、豪华富丽著称，
是过去"皇家的面子"。

京绣形成于明清，
融合各家绣法之所长。
"皇家血统"使京绣用材极尽奢华，
绣线除了有蚕丝制成的绒线，
还有金银锤箔捻成的金线，
千丝万缕之间透露着皇家气派。

中国人讲究个"好彩头"，
皇室更是如此。
京绣多以各类祥瑞图案为主题，
比如龙凤、珍禽异兽、花卉吉符等纹样。
用色与图案一样富有象征性，
每一种颜色都有不同的寓意。
黄色代表天子至高无上的权力；
红色代表喜庆与吉祥；
蓝色则是高雅尊贵的象征。
选色丰富多彩，配色又浑然一体。

京绣绘出了北京城独有的文化与记忆。
一针一线，
流露出中国古代的"匠人精神"。

补注·延伸

一片丝罗轻似水，洞房西室女工劳。花随玉指添春色，鸟逐金针长羽毛。蜀锦谩夸声自贵，越绫虚说价功高。可中用作鸳鸯被，红叶枝枝不碍刀。

——罗隐（唐）
《绣》

线蹙密密度金针，一一针针观世音。妙净庄严成相好，光明感应发身心。江横练色月浮水，雨灌华枝春在林。闻见可中超有路，普门处处许相寻。

——释正觉（宋）
《余姚胡氏绣观音求颂》

天时人事日相催，冬至阳生春又来。刺绣五纹添弱线，吹葭六琯动浮灰。岸容待腊将舒柳，山意冲寒欲放梅。云物不殊乡国异，教儿且覆掌中杯。

——杜甫（唐）
《小至》

针锋上直入，线缝里跳出。剪刀尺子自随身，号令乾坤齐万物。

——释咸杰（宋）
《赞绣宝公》

同、光间，首推京绣，有五彩、平金、拉索、打子之别。五彩尤精，一切花卉、山水、禽兽、鱼虫等，栩栩如生，呼之欲出，西人亦极赞之。

——徐珂（清）
《清稗类钞》

摘绫法如近日之摘棉，以甚薄之绫，摘成花朵之类而另以线缀于绣片之上……假如作梅花一枝，其枝干用平金或他法绣而以绫摘成花朵，以线缀之，其花蕊心则仍用针另行绣出。

——张华璂（清末民初）
《刺绣术》

Beijing Embroidery

扫码观看视频

These stunning flowers and birds are all works of Beijing embroidery, a traditional craft that has been passed down through generations.

Beijing embroidery is one of the eight exquisite handicrafts of Beijing. Also known as Imperial Embroidery, it was originally made for the imperial household.

Developing during China's last two dynasties (1368-1911), it was used to make luxurious imperial robes with silk thread as well as gold thread, symbolizing wealth and power.

Patterns of the Beijing embroidery depict auspicious things and signs, such as the Chinese dragon and phoenix as well as other auspicious animals and blooming flowers.

Different colors of the embroidery have different symbolic meanings. Yellow represents the emperors' supreme power. Red is festive and auspicious, whereas blue symbolizes elegance and dignity.

Various patterns and colors of Beijing embroidery are combined harmoniously, showing the spirit of Chinese craftsmen.

苗绣

苗　绣

扫码观看视频

你见过长着人脸的蝴蝶吗？
见过长着鱼尾的龙吗？
在苗绣中，一切皆有可能。
苗绣是苗族民间的刺绣技艺，
是苗族姑娘勤劳和智慧的结晶。

传说有位叫兰娟的女首领，
为了记住长途迁徙的路线，
想出了用彩线刺绣记路的法子。
她每每蹚水过河、翻山越岭，
都要在身上绣个符号标记，
等到了目的地，
全身从衣领到裤脚已全部绣满花纹。
从此，苗家姑娘出嫁，
都要穿上一身亲手绣制的盛装，
来继承前辈流传下的智慧与美丽。

如今苗绣的主题多源于
苗族的图腾崇拜，
蝴蝶纹、鸟纹、鱼纹和植物，
都是常见的纹样，
其中，蝴蝶纹最为重要。
苗族人相信，
"蝴蝶妈妈"作为人类始祖之一，
会庇佑她的子孙。

当然，必不可少的还有龙纹苗绣。
龙，是汉文化的象征，
代表着庄严与权威。
可在苗家姑娘的巧手下，
牛头、鱼身、鹰爪
都可以自由地加在苗龙上，
使传统的中国龙更添几分亲近、
可爱与民族特色。

苗绣不受传统刺绣的条理约束，
全凭苗族姑娘充沛的
想象和浪漫的才情。
让我们一起和苗绣
来一场天马行空的邂逅吧！

补注·延伸

继续实施传统工艺振兴计划，推动传统美术、传统技艺在现代生活中广泛应用，加强苗绣等传统纺染织绣项目的保护传承……加快推进苗绣产业高质量发展，壮大苗绣产业市场主体，研发生产高品质苗绣产品。

——中共贵州省委办公厅 贵州省人民政府办公厅
《关于进一步加强非物质文化遗产保护工作的实施意见》

织绩木皮，染以草实，好五色衣服，制裁皆有尾形……衣裳斑兰，语言侏离，好入山壑，不乐平旷。

——范晔（南北朝）
《后汉书·南蛮》

缋画，注凡绣亦须画，乃刺之；故画绣二工，共其职也。

——《周礼·冬官考工记》

苗民性喜彩衣，能织纫，有苗巾、苗锦之属。

——《永顺府志》（卷一）

怀远苗，男女服以青布绣花，极工巧。

——钱元昌（清）
《粤西诸蛮图记》

Miao Embroidery

扫码观看视频

Can you imagine a butterfly with a human face? Or a Chinese dragon with a fish tail? Such creative combinations occur in Miao embroidery. The Miao people are one of China's ethnic groups, famous for their craftsmanship.

Legend has it that a Miao heroine named Lanjuan, embroidered pictures on her dress as a way to record her people's migration routes. She marked different landmarks with different colored threads, and at the end of the journey, her dress was covered with beautiful intricate embroidery. Today, the embroidery is mainly used to adorn a Miao lady's ceremonial costume, like her wedding dress.

In Miao embroidery, nature motifs such as butterflies, birds, fish and flowers, frequently appear. In Miao mythology, the creator of all living things is the Butterfly Mother. So, butterflies are often depicted in Miao embroidery.

The Chinese dragon, a totem of the Han Chinese people, representing majesty and authority, also appears in Miao embroidery. The dragon with Miao characteristics combines the bull's head, the body with fish scales and the eagle's claws in an unconventional way, looking more approachable and adorable.

As one of China's state-level intangible cultural heritage items, Miao embroidery is filled with the Miao ladies' imagination and creativity.

苏 绣

扫码观看视频

一根银针在手中游走，
丝线在绸缎上翩翩起舞，
中国苏绣，以针作画，
勾勒江南之美。
苏绣是中国四大名绣之一，
起源于两千多年前的苏州。
苏绣按针法分为乱针绣与平绣，
可做单面绣、双面绣。
色彩清雅，绣工精细。

劈丝是苏绣处理丝线的独特方法，
劈出最细的丝线，
直径只有头发丝的十分之一，
一幅绣工精美的作品，
需要十几万次的穿针引线。
美物不易得，
针线之间考验的是极致的"匠心"。

传统的苏绣大多以中国工笔画为蓝本，
尤以花鸟和小动物为主，
最得意的是"小猫"和"金鱼"，
绰约亲昵之态跃然绣布之上。
今天的苏绣，博采众长，
融中西方绘画、摄影等
艺术形式于作品中。

中国苏绣纳天地自然，
集风月雅物于一针一线中，
呈现着中国文化和
艺术技艺的博大精深。
绣出来的山水能分远近之趣，
楼阁具现深邃之体，
人物能有瞻眺生动之情，
栩栩如生的苏绣
带来了惊艳世界的东方美学。

补注·延伸

晋平公使叔向聘于吴，吴人拭舟以逆之，左五百人，右五百人，有绣衣而豹裘者，有锦衣而狐裘者。

——刘向（汉）
《说苑》

宋人之绣，针线细密，用绒止一二丝。用针如发细者为之，设色精妙，光彩射目。

——董其昌（明）
《筠清轩秘录》

日暮堂前花蕊娇，争拈小笔上床描。绣成安向春园里，引得黄莺下柳条。

——胡令能（唐）
《观郑州崔郎中诸妓绣样》

Suzhou Embroidery

扫码观看视频

A silver needle moving with the hand while the thread dancing on the silk, Chinese *suxiu* (Suzhou Embroidery) uses needles to paint the beauty of Jiangnan (the south of the Yangtze River). *Suxiu* is one of the four famous embroideries in China, originating in ancient Suzhou. *Suxiu* is divided into "random stitch" and "flat stitch". Artisans can make single-sided or double-sided embroidery in elegant colors.

Flying stitches endows *Suxiu* with the charm of poetry. Silk splitting is a unique method of processing thread in *suxiu*. The artisans split the thread to the thinnest, only one-tenth of human hair. An exquisite piece of embroidery needs thousands of stitches. Creating beauty requires diligence. The ultimate "ingenuity" is tested in every stitch.

Most of the traditional *suxiu* designs are based on Chinese brush paintings, such as flowers, birds and small animals. The most outstanding are "kitten" and "goldfish", which are recreated with a delicate and intimate look. Today's *suxiu* has integrated Chinese and Western painting, photography and other art forms into the works.

Chinese *suxiu* blends the natural beauty into stitches. It is the masterpiece of Chinese culture and artistic skills, in which the landscape can be distinguished between the distant and near and the characters have vivid expressions. Suzhou embroidery brings the amazing Chinese aesthetics to the world.

挑 花

扫码观看视频

刺绣一定是五颜六色、
轻薄柔软的吗？
中国挑花就不拘泥于此。
看，这块朴素的麻布上，
几只用白线挑绣的大公鸡威风凛凛。
挑花是我国传统的手工技艺，
也是各地挑花艺人们代代相传的绝技。

不同针法制作出的
挑花绣品各具特色。
"挑"出来的挑花，
图案细腻，正反一致。
"钻"出来的钻花，
图案立体、栩栩如生。
姑娘们亲手制作的挑花绣品，
不仅可以装点生活，
更是送给心上人的信物，
象征着浪漫的爱情与思念。

挑花丰富多样的图案，
大都源于日常生活。
比如花瑶人民长期生活在
山深林密的环境中，湿热多蛇，
所以在花瑶挑花中蛇图案最为常见。
一针一线，饱含了花瑶人民
图腾信仰下对生活的热爱。

生活中丰富的元素在刺绣艺人的
巧手中"挑、钻、游、织"，
活灵活现地呈现在绣布上。

挑花，三分传承，七分创造。
一针一线
挑出中国传统刺绣工艺的独特魅力。

解码中华文化基因

补注·延伸

莹莹手巾四四方,挑个明月照花墙,外面挑个郎望姐,里面挑个姐望郎。

——《挑花歌》

积绩木皮,染以草实,好五色衣服。

——应劭(汉)

《风俗通义》

长沙郡杂有夷蜒,名曰"莫瑶",其女子蓝布衫,斑布裙,通无鞋履。

——魏征(唐)

《隋书》

Chinese Cross Stitch

扫码观看视频

Do you think embroidery must be multicolored, thin, and soft? No, Chinese cross-stitching works show its uniqueness. Look at this linen! Simple white threads give life to the vibrant roosters. Chinese cross stitch, also named tiaohua, is a traditional handicraft passed down through generations.

Embroidery with different stitching styles have their own characteristics. The stitch of "picking" makes the same intricate pattern on both sides of the fabric, while the "drilled" flowers have three-dimensional and lifelike patterns. The cross stitch embroidery made by girls can not only decorate people's home, but also be used as keepsakes for their beloved, symbolizing romantic love and missing.

The rich and diverse patterns of cross stitch mostly come from daily life. For example, the image of snakes is common in Huayao cross stitch, because Huayao people live in hot and humid areas where snakes are often seen. Huayao people sew their totemic belief and love for life into their works.

Through exquisite stitching work, artisans depict their life vividly on the fabrics. Cross stitch, a combination of inheritance and creativity, shows the special charm of traditional Chinese embroidery.

北京玉雕

北京玉雕

扫码观看视频

中国人自古对玉器情有独钟，
玉石文化传承至今已有八千年的历史，
玉雕就是从玉制具发展而来的。
清代南方匠人到北京传艺，
由此北京玉雕集南北之所长，
吸收宫廷技艺，
形成了料实工精、
设计大方的"京作流派"。

北京玉雕的制作玉料种类繁多，
常见的有和田玉、翡翠、玛瑙等十大类。
民间的能工巧匠擅长因材施艺，
根据不同玉料的自然形状与色泽纹路
创作出各具特色的珍品。
北京玉雕题材更是广泛，
有栩栩如生的人物、花卉、鸟、兽，
也有别具一格的首饰、器皿、盆景、盆花。
不同主题的玉雕工艺各不相同，
真让人眼花缭乱，美不胜收。

玉雕不仅仅具有美学价值，
历代的思想家和文人
给玉注入了丰富的文化内涵。
中国古人说"玉不琢，不成器"，
只有历经雕琢，才有这精美的玉雕，
只有历经磨难，人才能成才。
"谦谦君子，温润如玉"
已深深融入中国人的血脉之中，
构成了璀璨的中华文化。

补注·延伸

雍州贡琳琅，扬州贡瑶琨。

——《书经·禹贡篇》

如果用一种物质代表中华文化，那就是玉。

——季羡林

温润而泽，仁也；缜密以栗，知也。

——《礼记·聘义》

石崇富比王家，当世珍宝奇异，皆殊方异国所得。其爱婢翔风妙别玉声，悉知其处。言西北方玉声沉重，而性温润，东方南方玉声轻洁，而性清凉。其言玉声清洁者，言东南方产非真玉也。

——王嘉（晋）
《拾遗记》

勃律天西采玉河，坚昆碧碗最来多，旧随汉使千堆宝，少答胡王万匹罗。

——杜甫（唐）
《喜闻盗贼蕃寇总退口号五首》

Beijing Jade Carving

扫码观看视频

Chinese people have been fond of jade since ancient times. The jade culture has a history of 8,000 years. Jade carving is developed from jade ware.

In the 17th century (Qing Dynasty), southern craftsmen came to Beijing, and thus the Beijing jade carving gathered the strengths of the north and south.

Various types of jade are used in Beijing Jade carving, including Hetian jade, jadeite and agate. Skilled craftsmen know how to create distinctive treasures based on the original shape, color, texture of the jade.

The designs of jade works vary considerably, from characters, flowers, birds, beasts, to jewelry, utensils, bonsai, and potted flowers. The themes were accompanied by the distinctive carving of the craftsmen.

Jade carving has aesthetic value, and the intellectuals have injected rich cultural connotations into jade.

As the ancient Chinese saying goes, "A jade without polishing is useless." Only after polishing, can there be an exquisite jade artwork. likewise, only through overcoming adversities, can a man become strong.

With a rich heritage and ongoing innovation in jade craftsmanship, the cultural value and designs will reach new hights in the future.

石 雕

扫码观看视频

一枚小小的石头，
镌刻着历史的层层纹理。
诞生于人类"婴孩时期"的石雕艺术，
正无声地讲述着
数千年来人们的奇思妙想。

四川省乐山市南岷江东岸，
一尊高达 71 米的佛像
安静地伫立了上千年。
历经风吹日晒，
大佛表面已遍布岁月的痕迹。
然而，这尊建自唐朝开元年间的石佛，
却只是石雕艺术的后来者。
早在遥远的石器时代，
山顶洞人就将石头琢磨穿孔，
制成装饰品。
自此，随处可见的石料
成了人类攻无不克的雕刻质材，
石雕艺术也应运而生。

中国的石雕艺人们讲究
"因材而施艺，因色而取巧"，
石头天然的纹理和色泽
是石雕最终成形的关键。
一块"颜值在线"的石头被匠人相中，
经过设计、凿胚、修光、上油等环节，
便会脱下粗糙的外衣，
进化成圆滑莹润的石雕作品。
看那栩栩如生的菊花石雕，
晶莹剔透的寿山石雕，
还有壮观恢宏的大足石雕，
一块块山中璞石，在匠人的巧手之下，
变换各种造型，达到天工合一的境界。

大匠运斤，顽石雕琢生花，
不着点墨，尽显天然本色。
石雕是创造与重生的艺术，
它默默不语，
却承载了人与自然的永恒记忆。

补注·延伸

其雕镌制度有四等：一曰剔地起突；二曰压地隐起华；三曰减地平钑；四曰素平。

——李诫（宋）
《营造法式》

端州石工巧如神，踏天磨刀割紫云。佣刓抱水含满唇，暗洒苌弘冷血痕。

——李贺（唐）
《杨生青花紫石砚歌》

Stone Carving

扫码观看视频

A small stone is engraved with layers of history. The art of stone carving was born in the early days of mankind. It is silently telling the fancies of human beings for thousands of years.

On the east bank of the Min River in the south of Leshan City, Sichuan Province, a 71-meter-high Buddha statue has been standing quietly for more than a thousand years. The surface of the Buddha has been covered with traces of time in the wind and sun. However, this stone Buddha built in the 8th century is only a latecomer to the art of stone carving. As early as the Stone Age, the Upper Cave Men polished and pierced stones for decoration. Since then, the stone has become an excellent material for carving, and stone carving art hereby emerged.

Chinese stone artists carve in accordance with the natural texture and color of the stone, which is the key to the final shape of the stone carving. They select a piece of "good-looking" stone, and after designing, chiseling, polishing and oiling, the artists finally take off the rough coat of the raw material and turn it into a work of art. Look at the intensely vivid chrysanthemum stone carving, the crystal Shoushan stone carving, and the magnificent Dazu stone carving. Common stones are transformed into various shapes by the craftsmen to achieve a unity of nature and craftsmanship.

Stone carving is the art of creation and rebirth, which silently carries the eternal memory of human and nature.

贝 雕

扫码观看视频

当一枚平凡的贝壳遇到它的"伯乐",
会焕发出怎样的光华?
从贝壳到贝雕的华丽转身,
是大自然的鬼斧神工
与精巧手艺的奇妙碰撞。

中国人与贝壳的渊源由来已久。
早在山顶洞人时期,
先祖们就把贝链当作装饰。
商代以后,贝壳还充当了货币的角色。
秦汉年间,
人们在贝壳上雕出简单的鸟兽图样,
镶嵌在器皿、桌椅等器物上,
称之为"螺钿",
这便是贝雕的前身。
经过历代匠人的传承与发展,
融合了牙雕、玉雕、木雕及国画的灵感,
贝雕艺术被注入了新的活力。

来自江河湖海的贝壳
经选材、绘画、雕琢等多个工序,
就能摇身一变成为精美的工艺品。
红色的海螺、鸡心螺可以制成枫叶,
海红贝的独特斑痕可以雕琢为古树,
黑色螺旋纹贝壳妆点仕女的发髻,
江贝的层层纹理化作曼妙衣裙……
千姿百态的贝壳在匠人的巧手下
成就了无数巧夺天工的贝雕作品,
闪耀着天然的质感和人类智慧的光辉。

亿万年前,我们从大海走来,
贝雕作为海之绮丽与人类技艺的结晶,
每一件作品都承载着
古老文化与现代文明,
讲述着人类与海洋的动人故事。

补注·延伸

缀珠陷钿贴云母,五金七宝相玲珑。

——白居易(唐)
《三谣·素屏谣》

(螺钿)又分截壳色,随彩而施缀者,光华可赏。

——《髹饰录》

螺钿器皿,元时富家不限年月做造。

——《格古要论》

天光白毫际,山色钿螺边。

——宋祁(宋)
《大像阁》

Shell Carving

扫码观看视频

What brilliance will it have when a shell encounters a craftsman? The gorgeous change from a shell to a shell carving is a wonderful collision of nature and human's exquisite craftsmanship.

Chinese people have a long-standing relationship with shells. As early as the caveman period, ancestors used the shell chains as decorations. After the Shang Dynasty (1600BC-1046BC), shells also served as currency. During the Qin (221BC-207BC) and Han Dynasties (206BC-220AD), shells carved with simple bird and beast patterns, called luodian, were inlaid on utensils, and they were the early shell carvings. After the inheritance and development of craftsmen, and combined with ivory, jade, wood carving and Chinese painting, the art of shell carving is bursting with new vitality.

Shells from rivers, lakes and seas, after selection, painting, and carving, can be transformed into exquisite handicrafts. Red sea snails can be made into maple leaves; the ridges on red sea shells are ideal lines for ancient tree leaves; the black spiral shells decorate the buns of ladies; and the textures of river shells can be turned into graceful dresses... In the skillful hands of craftsmen, various shells become countless exquisite shell carvings, glowing with natural texture and human wisdom.

Billions of years ago, human life originated in the sea. As the perfect combination of the beauty of the sea and human skills, each piece of shell carving carries ancient culture and modern civilization, and tells the touching stories between man and the ocean...

竹刻

竹 刻

扫码观看视频

中国是世界上最早使用竹子的国家，
竹刻艺术应时而生。
细致的刀工和精妙的纹饰，
成就了竹刻独树一帜的艺术风格。

中国竹刻早在商朝前就已出现，
远古的先民们
将符号刻在竹子上来记事。
自西周起，
竹简、竹扇等竹制品便风行一时。
到了宋代，
竹刻的艺术性与观赏性逐渐增强，
建筑、人物、花鸟等元素
成为雕刻的主题。
明清时期，
竹刻艺术空前发展，达到鼎盛，
出现了许多雕刻精细、
古朴雅致的艺术精品。

几千年来，竹刻艺术发展出多个流派，
不同流派的艺术风格各具特色。

嘉定竹刻以深刀见长，
将书法、绘画、诗文、雕刻
巧妙地融为一体，
赋予竹新的生命。
金陵竹刻则以浅刻闻名，
寥寥数刀就能刻画出深远的意境。
浙派竹刻工于留青，
素雅淡泊，余韵无穷。
徽州竹刻因材施艺，
突破传统小器限制，
使大件竹刻成为可能。
每一件竹刻作品
都浓缩了雕刻艺人的匠心，
展示了自古以来匠人们的巧思和智慧。

竹，是君子的化身，
从泥泞中走来，傲立于天地间。
千百年来的雕刻艺人
将竹的气节深深地
刻进了中华文化的基因，
诉说着中国人的情怀。

补注·延伸

四面皆花板，皆于竹片上刻成宫室、人物、山水、花木、禽鸟、纤悉俱备。其细若缕，而且玲珑活动，求之数百年，无复此一人矣！

——陶宗仪（元末明初）

《南村辍耕录》

凡云气、夕阳、炊烟，皆就竹皮之色为之。妙造自然，不类刻画。

——李葆恂（清末民初）

《旧学庵笔记》

笏，天子以球玉，诸侯以象，大夫以鱼须文竹，士竹本象可也。……凡有指画于君前，用笏造，受命于君前，则书于笏，笏毕用也，因饰焉。

——《礼记·玉藻》

Bamboo Carving

扫码观看视频

China is the first country in the world to use bamboo, giving rise to the art of bamboo carving. The meticulous carving skills and exquisite patterns have contributed to the unique artistic style of bamboo carving.

Chinese bamboo carving has been in existence since the 17th century BC when the ancient people carved signs on bamboo to record things. Since the 11th century BC, bamboo products like bamboo slips and bamboo fans had gained in popularity. In the Song Dynasty (960-1279), the artistry and ornamental value of bamboo carving gradually increased, and elements such as figures, flowers and birds became the themes of carving. From the 14th century to early 20th century, the unprecedented development of bamboo carving reached its climax, and many elegantly carved works of art emerged.

For thousands of years, the art of bamboo carving has developed into several schools, each with its distinctive artistic style. Jiading bamboo carving is known for its deep carving. It skillfully integrates calligraphy, painting, poetry and carving, giving bamboo a new life. Jinling bamboo carving is known for its shallow relief carving, which creates a profound artistic conception with just a few cuts. Zhejiang bamboo carving strives for keeping the primary color of bamboo to present simplicity and elegance. Huizhou bamboo carving makes a breakthrough from the traditional limitation of small pieces to make large bamboo carving possible. These artworks show the ingenuity of craftsmen since ancient times.

Bamboo, the embodiment of the gentleman, comes from mud and stands tall in the world. For thousands of years, carving artists have deeply engraved bamboo's temperament into the genes of Chinese culture, telling the feelings of Chinese people.

泉州木雕

扫码观看视频

以木为纸，以刀代笔，
中国工匠用一双巧手
让小小木头身价百倍，
这其中的门道还得从泉州木雕说起。
泉州木雕是福建民间工艺的代表，
小到木偶小像，大到家具建筑，
都可以用木头雕刻而成。

泉州木雕起源于唐代，
到明清时期技术逐渐纯熟，
安海龙山寺里至今仍保留着
一尊明朝的佳作——千手观音，
作品整体由一棵樟树雕刻而成。
这尊木雕观音共有1008只手，
分别拿着书卷、钟鼓、珠宝等各种法器，
手势也各不相同。
每只手的手心位置都雕有一只眼睛，
千手千眼寓意遍观世间、庇护众生。

木雕的制作流程并不复杂，
却极考验匠人的技巧与耐心。
先用笔在木头上画出形状，
再用不同刀具将多余部分剔除，
重复多次，不断细化，
最后用砂纸打磨光滑。
最困难也是最难得之处
是要依照木头本来的纹路设计造型，
需要综合运用镂空雕刻、
浮雕、浅雕等多类技法，
这样的木雕才能
既美观自然又大方实用。

如今的3D建模技术，
使得工艺品的制作成本大大降低，
却少了那种精心雕琢的工匠精神。
让我们回归初心，
跟随泉州木雕来感受美吧！

补注·延伸

君不见峄山高崖斯相迹，枣木刻模真并失。又不见深之袖手安国碑，帝悟百牛欣倒石。秦唐二子皆有声，何必今人不逾昔。拙工砺器雕不已，印版传书差可贵。方趺图首效碑影，穿凿胶黏总纰颣。凤山之水生琼玖，斯磨光泽坚而黝。文章光艳照千古，玉牒万金吁可剖。刊劂四海多名手，何必区区镌腐朽。

——苏籀（宋）
《雕木工》

商人白有功言：在泺口河上，见一人荷竹簏，牵巨犬二。于簏中出木雕美人，高尺余，手目转动，艳妆如生。又以小锦鞯被犬身，便令跨座。安置已，叱犬疾奔。美人自起，学解马作诸剧，镫而腹藏，腰而尾赘，跪拜起立，灵变无讹。又作昭君出塞，别取一木雕儿，插雉尾，披羊裘，跨犬从之。昭君频频回顾，羊裘儿扬鞭追逐，真如生者。

——蒲松龄（清）
《聊斋志异》

Quanzhou Wood Carving

扫码观看视频

With wood as paper and knife as pen, Chinese craftsmen use their hands to make wood highly valuable. Quanzhou wood carving is a representative of Fujian folk arts. From small statues to large furniture or even architecture, many things can be carved from wood.

Quanzhou wood carving originated in the Tang Dynasty (618-907), and gradually became a mature craftsmanship after the 15th century. In the Longshan Temple, there is still a masterpiece— "Thousand-Hand Guanyin", made in the Ming Dynasty (1368-1644). The whole work is carved from one camphor tree. The wood-carved Guanyin statue has 1008 hands, holding scrolls, bells, drums, jewelry and so on, with different gestures. There is an eye carved in the palm of each hand, which means watching the world and protecting all sentient beings.

The production process of wood carving is not complicated, but it is a test of craftsmen's skills and patience. First draw the shape on the wood, and then carve away material with different tools. This step has to be repeated many times, and finally the work needs to be polished with sand paper. The most difficult part is to design according to the original wood grain. Various techniques, such as hollow carving, embossing and bas-relief, will be used to make wood carving works beautiful and useful.

Today's 3D modeling technology has greatly reduced the cost of making handicrafts, but it lacks artisan's spirit to continuously elaborate. Let's try to feel the beauty of Quanzhou wood carving!

泥 塑

扫码观看视频

看，这个小女孩，
脸蛋红扑扑，身穿一件大花袄，
是不是精致可爱，栩栩如生？
她叫"梦娃"，是一件中国泥塑。

泥塑是中国传统美术品。
传说千万年前，天地初开，
神创造了日月星辰、飞禽走兽，
可大地依旧冷清，
女娲便用黄土和成泥，
照着自己的样子，
捏出了许多小泥娃娃，
于是就有了最早的人类。

在民间，泥塑内涵丰富，
寄托着普通百姓朴素美好的愿望。
白泥娃娃，寓意早生贵子，
小孩白白胖胖；
老虎娃娃，寓意生龙活虎，

小孩健康平安。

经过历代传承与发展，
传统泥塑分为了众多流派。
惠山泥人，色彩鲜明，
乡土气息浓郁；
凤翔泥塑，造型夸张，
神情憨态可掬；
天津有大名鼎鼎的"泥人张"，
源于清代，
至今已有一百八十余年的历史，
他的手艺号称"触手成像"，
技艺高深、惟妙惟肖。

泥塑讲述的是生活的故事，
每一件泥塑作品
都体现着中国艺人对生活
细致入微的观察，
他们用泥土呈现出了丰富多彩的世界。

补注·延伸

用泥土凝固客家风情,留给千秋万代。

——潘鹤

至其如何工作?不过在观戏时,即以台上角色,权当模特儿,端详相貌,剔取特征,于人不知不觉中,袖中暗地摹索。一出未终,而伶工像成;归而敷粉涂色,衬以衣冠,即能丝毫不爽。

——《大公报》

色雅而简,至其比例之精确、骨格之肯定、与其传神之微妙,据我在北方所见美术作品中,只有历代帝王中宋太祖、太宗之像可比拟之。若在雕刻中,虽杨惠之不足多也。

——徐悲鸿
《大陆杂志》

Clay Figurines

扫码观看视频

Look at this red-cheek little girl in a big floral jacket! Isn't she lovely? Her name is "Mengwa", and she is a Chinese clay figurine.

Clay figurines are traditional Chinese artworks. It is said that thousands of years ago, after the creation of the sun, the moon, the stars and beasts, a goddess named Nüwa was still unsatisfied with the desolation, so she used loess and water to make many little clay figures that looked like her. They became the earliest humans.

As folk art, clay figurines have rich connotations, representing the simple and good wishes of common people. For example, a white clay doll implies the blessing for couples to have a cute baby while a tiger doll means the wish for kids to be healthy and strong.

Based on the techniques passed down from ancestors, traditional clay figurines can be divided into many schools. Huishan clay figurines feature the bright colors and country style. Fengxiang clay figurines have exaggerated shapes and cute looks. In Tianjin, the well-known "Clay Figurine Zhang" originated from the Qing Dynasty (1644-1911) and has a history of more than 180 years. He is praised for his expressive deftness to sculpt lifelike figures.

With clay, Chinese artisans show their close observation of life and present our colorful world.

安溪竹藤编

扫码观看视频

中国人爱竹,
中国文人"宁可食无肉,
不可居无竹"。
中华传统工艺安溪竹藤编
将竹藤编织成各种各样的精美器具,
让竹常伴人们身边。

安溪竹藤编工艺历史悠久,
早在宋元时期就十分普及,
人们大量使用竹藤编制农具、
茶具等生活用品,
如竹箱、斗箕、蒸笼等。

竹藤编的主要原料是毛竹、
木料和各种藤类。
编织过程中,
纵向的线条为"经",
横向的线条为"纬",
相互挑压交织,纵横交错。
通过立体或平面的编织技法,
时而密编,时而疏编,
延伸出众多编织花样。

看,这件竹藤编作品《云锦瓶》,
由薄如纸片的竹篾丝
编织而成。
结构优雅结实、花纹立体细致,
充分体现了安溪竹藤编工艺
精致美观、大方实用的特点。

千百年来,
安溪竹藤编不断突破创新。
不仅成了当地的支柱产业,
更让古老的技艺
在今天焕发出蓬勃活力。

补注·延伸

坐肆列邸,贸通有无;荷畚执筐,为安职业。

——詹敦仁（后梁）
《五代初建安溪县记》

漳州描金漆杯,用竹丝编成,又有茶盘俱耐用。

——《福州通志》

良工眇芳林,妙思触物骋。箑疑秋蝉翼,团取望舒景。

——许询（晋）
《竹扇诗》

Anxi Bamboo and Rattan Weaving

扫码观看视频

Chinese people love bamboo. Chinese literati wrote many poems for bamboo. (e.g. rather eat without meat than live without bamboo.) Chinese craftsmen (Anxi bamboo and rattan weaving) weave bamboo and rattan into various fine tools, turning bamboo into a constant companion for Chinese people.

This craft in Anxi County dates back to the 10th–14th century (Song and Yuan Dynasties). People made bamboo and rattan into agricultural tools, tea sets and other necessities, such as bamboo boxes, dustpans and steamers.

The main raw materials are bamboo, wood and various types of rattan. The vertical lines, called "warp", and the horizontal lines, called "weft", are intertwined and crisscrossed to make a bamboo work. Through flat or 3D weaving techniques, either densely or sparsely woven, the lines can be made into various patterns.

Look at this vase, Cloud Brocade Vase. It is woven by paper-thin bamboo strips. The elegant structure and detailed 3D pattern fully reflect the beautiful and practical features of this art.

This craft becomes a local pillar industry for Anxi County, and continues to flourish today.

香 包

扫码观看视频

细腻柔软，小巧玲珑，芳香扑鼻，
眼前这个精致的荷包就是中国香包。
绣着各式图案的彩绸里，
包裹着多种气味芳香的中草药细末。
香包，真可谓"秀外慧中"。

早在约三千年前就有了香包。
人们在蚊虫盛行时，
会把艾草、雄黄和檀香等香料、
药材的粉末装在小布袋里，
给小孩和老人佩戴，
防止他们被毒虫侵扰。
自那时起，
驱邪祈福就成了香包的主题。

香包的制作工艺独特，
尤以绣工精美见长，
设计以出新、出奇为特色。
色彩搭配对比强烈，
形状多样、不拘一格，
有心形、元宝形、蝴蝶形，
还有花瓶形和水滴形等。
不同形状和内料的香包，
演变出多种功能和内涵。
刺绣精致的可以用来
装饰衣着、把玩欣赏；
填有药材的
则多具有安神醒脑等实用功效；
古书记载，
大户人家的未成年子女
拜见父母时也需佩戴香包，
可见香包也有礼仪上的功能。

香包的图案也极为丰富。
有长辈青睐的梅花、菊花等吉祥图饰，
也有小朋友喜爱的动物图案，
如果是热恋中的情人，那就更加讲究了，
姑娘们会精心绣制一枚别致的香包，
让它常伴心上人左右。

小小的香包为我们的生活
带来多少情趣和温馨啊！

补注·延伸

扈江篱与辟芷兮，纫秋兰以为佩。

——屈原（战国时期）
《离骚》

拂胸轻粉絮，暖手小香囊。

——白居易（唐）
《江南喜逢萧九彻因话长安旧游戏赠五十韵》

何以致叩叩？香囊系肘后。

——繁钦（汉）
《定情诗》

男女未冠笄者，鸡初鸣，咸盥漱，栉縰，拂髦，总角，衿缨，皆佩容臭，昧爽而朝，问何食饮矣。若已食则退；若未食则佐长者视具。

——《礼记·内则》

红罗复斗帐，四角垂香囊。

——《孔雀东南飞》

Chinese Sachets

扫码观看视频

Delicate and soft, small and aromatic, the scented bag in front of you is a Chinese sachet. Embroidered with different patterns, packed with various fragrant herbal powder, sachets can be described as "beautiful outside, bountiful inside".

Three thousand years ago, people packed the powder of spices and medicinal herbs (wormwood, realgar, and sandalwood) into small cloth bags for children and the elderly to repel poisonous insects. Since then, the sachets have been applied to ward off evil spirits and pray for good fortune.

Sachets are created with unique methods (exquisite embroidery). The design is novel and innovative. The colors are in striking contrast. The shapes are diverse and unconventional, such as heart, ingot, butterfly, or vase and waterdrop... Sachets of different shapes and fillings have various functions. Those with delicate embroidery can decorate clothes. The ones filled with herbs have practical functions (soothing the nerves and refreshing the brain). In ancient books, children of wealthy families also wore sachets when they greeted their parents, which shows the ritual function of sachets.

The graphics on the sachets are also rich. Plum blossoms and chrysanthemums are auspicious patterns favored by the elders, and animal patterns are loved by children. Girls in love will carefully embroider a charming sachet and give it to their lovers as a token of love.

Those small sachets can bring so much fun and warmth to our life!

北京绢花

扫码观看视频

姹紫嫣红总是春,
但是有种花儿却能够四季不败。
这就是北京绢花,也叫"京花",
是老北京传统的彩扎艺术。
京城人的记忆里,
大都有绢花绚烂的身影。

北京绢花是用各种颜色的丝织品
制作的花卉。
早在一千七百多年前,
中国就已经出现这种技艺。
相传唐代杨贵妃四季都要簪花,
用花朵遮挡鬓角的疤痕。
待到寒冬时节,百花凋零,
便用绫绸做成假花代替。
北京绢花从元代定都北京后,
逐渐兴盛起来。
绢花的用途非常广泛,
在民间的婚丧嫁娶和寿诞等
喜庆的节日中,
绢花都扮演着重要的角色。

绢花的制作工艺精细、复杂,
工匠们精心选择多种丝织物为原料,
先制成花瓣、花蕊、花叶,
再把它们粘成花朵,
攒成一枝枝完整的花束,
组合为成品。
在绢花匠人的巧手下,
秋菊清雅,杜鹃娇艳,梅花秀丽,
各色花卉栩栩如生、以假乱真,
将刹那芳华长久保留在人间。

如今,北京绢花的品种
已经发展到两千多种,
北京绢花来源于生活,
又装点了生活。
在萧瑟的冬日里,
营造出百花争艳的景象,
给人们带来春天的希望。

补注·延伸

彼时旗汉妇女戴花成为风习，其中尤以梳旗头之妇女最喜色彩鲜艳、花样新奇的人造花。

——汤用彬
《旧都文物略》

花儿市中多市花，市花五色人前夸，……富家生女称国色，一花三日插不得，贫家无米愁炊烟，女儿买花不惜钱。

——张祥和
《花市儿歌》

Beijing Silk Flowers

扫码观看视频

Most flowers only bloom in spring, but in Beijing there's one kind that can last forever—the Beijing silk flowers. It's one of China's national-level intangible cultural heritage items, adding more colors to people's life.

In China, silk fabric of different colors was used, over 1,700 years ago, to make floral hair pins. Legend has it that one of the Four Beauties of ancient China, Yang Guifei (719-756), always decorated her hair with flowers. In winter, she would use flowers made of silk.

The Beijing silk flowers became popular in the Yuan Dynasty (1206-1368) over 700 years ago. The silk flowers have been used in various rituals and ceremonies including memorials, weddings and birthday parties.

The making of Beijing silk flowers involves quite complicated processes. A variety of silk fabric is made into different parts of the flowers which are then glued together to form a beautiful bouquet. These elegant chrysanthemums, exquisite azaleas and ethereal plum blossoms are all made by skillful Beijing silk flower artisans, who create beauty that is everlasting.

Today, more than 2,000 types of Beijing silk flower have been created. These dainty silk flowers decorate people's life in winter with vibrant and vivid colors, symbolizing the hope of spring.

后　记

　　本书的编创得到了中国传媒大学铸牢中华民族共同体意识研究基地的大力支持。中国新闻社充分发挥国内外传播的渠道优势，为视频作品的推广提供了优质平台。本书所收录的中英文版文稿、视频和交互程序，皆由中国传媒大学电视学院数字出版师生团队编创，详细名单附后。

文案统筹：

李艾珂、汤　璇、周晓萌、刘　雯、尚京华、李泓江

文案写作：

李怡滢、杨雨千、曲　伸、杨　宁、谭兰惠、王译丰、
刘　微、郭　玥、兰雅婷、陆昱颖、王晨祎、岳冀萌、
张绮月、郭书畅、黄影飞、陈　毅、汪　蕾、吴　蕾

视觉统筹：

曹航宇、孙洪亮、李尽沙

视频制作：

卜欣荣、徐远在、傅柏燃、宋依黛、袁志恒、吴梦涵、王伊鸣、
刘　瑶、蒙佳慧、袁嘉敏、张李偲、邓　石、臧英彤、钟　睿、

蒲诗钰、秦添天、田欣怡、杨子轶、宋翔堃、陈　超、黄睿思、
刘慧雯、卢肖依、曲　伸、任　艾、刘佳琪、霍逸凡、阮思羽、
丛　榕、王博麟

音频统筹：
蔡　雨

音频制作：
温莫寒、刘　琦、陈中瑞、张　竞、周　迅、高艺轩、徐劢航

交互统筹：
孙竞舟

交互制作：
陈姿璇、许潆珊